The
___ Militarists ___

Also by Edwin P. Hoyt

The Militarists

The Rise of Japanese Militarism Since WW II

by Edwin P. Hoyt

DONALD I. FINE, INC.   NEW YORK

Library of Congress Catalogue Card Number: 84-073520
ISBN: 0-917657-17-9
Manufactured in the United States of America
10 9 8 7 6 5 4 3 2 1

This book is printed on acid free paper. The paper in this book meets the guidelines for permanence and durability of the Committee on Production Guidelines for Book Longevity of the Council on Library Resources.

Grateful acknowledgment is made to the Japanese Defense Agency for permission to reprint the following numbered photos: 4, 7-10, 12-18, 22-30, and 32-34.

This book is dedicated to Hamako and Hiroko Hattori, two friends of mine who represent the old Japan (my generation) and the new (my children's generation).

Contents

ACKNOWLEDGMENTS

I am indebted to a large number of people for assistance and information in the research for this book. More or less in the order of contact they include: Admiral Arleigh Burke, USN (Ret.); Kakuko Shōji, of the University of Hawaii; Minoru Shōji, of Hawaii *Hochi*; Robert C. Miller of Hilo, Hawaii; Diana Hoyt of Washington, D.C.; Kumiko Yokoyama and Hiroko Hattori of the Tokyo public schools; Major General Yoshio Ishikawa, defense attaché at the Japanese embassy, Washington, D.C.; Robert Reck and Chris Bates of the U.S. Department of Commerce, Washington, D.C.; Commander Fred Leeder, USN; U.S. Department of Defense Public Information Office, Washington, D.C.; Public Information Office, U.S. Naval Academy, Annapolis, Md.; William Lenderking and Warren Magruder, U.S. Department of State, and half a dozen other officers who passed me from one to the other with no information; Takehisa Imaizumi, deputy chief, public information, Japan Defense Agency; Masuo Moritomi, director of public information, Japan Defense Agency; Seiichi Soeda and Shigeyoshi Araki, Foreign Press Center, Tokyo; Captain Walter Nix, U.S. defense attaché, U.S. embassy, Tokyo; Kiyohiko Koike, director, administrative department, National Defense Academy, Yokosuka, Japan; John Yamanaka, senior editor, and Kunichiro Suzuki, managing editor, the *Japan Times*; Masanori Katoh and Yoshitomo Sano, assistant chiefs, International Affairs Bureau, Komeito; Tsuneo Misawa, front office manager, Hotel Kayu Kaikan, Tokyo; Lieutenant Commander Shigeo Hayashi, JMSDF, Eta Jima; Colonel Satsumasu Kodama, JASDF; Lieutenant Colonel Mitsuo Sakudo, JGSDF, Tokyo; Colonel Nobumasa Tanaka, chief, Foreign Liaison Section, JASDF, Tokyo; Colonel Shigetaka Hasegawa, JGSDF; Colonel Mamoru Sato, JASADF; Takashi Kaise, SDF; Captain Koshori Fuyutsume, JGSDF.

As always, I am in debt to my wife and partner in all my literary excursions, Olga G. Hoyt, for research, editing and acceptance of many vicissitudes. In this case, at least, she got a trip to Japan.

The
—— Militarists ——

1
The Danger

Look ahead from now to the year 2001. The United States and the Union of Soviet Socialist Republics are at their usual squabbling over a disarmament that neither really wants. China, having exerted patience for many years over the Taiwan issue, has grown steadily more restless. The return of Hong Kong in the 1980s has backfired; China has secured sovereignty, but most of the international business firms that had chosen Hong Kong as headquarters have moved to places they consider more stable and more friendly to business: some to Tokyo, some to Singapore, some as far afield as Bermuda.

A rearmed Japan, by now pushed by the United States into the support of a navy of three hundred ships, a million-man army and a large air force, dominates the western Pacific Basin except for the Chinese mainland.

A serious recession in the 1990s has caused the United States to invoke paralyzing import penalties on Japanese automobiles, optics, computer sciences and other high technology. The result has been a serious economic depression in Japan; for, as always, she faces the old problem: high population density and virtually no raw materials except water power. The goodwill between Japan and the United States has evaporated as certainly as has Article IX of the Japanese constitution, that constitution written so long ago by the Americans and pushed on Japan, and for the same reason: the American failure to understand the Japanese.

In 2000 China and Japan strike a deal: The Japanese navy and air force will protect a Chinese landing on Taiwan. The Japanese and Chinese will lead a new Greater East Asia Co-Prosperity Sphere, which will bring peace and prosperity to Asians and make them independent of the economic colonialism of the super-powers. Japan will be the acknowledged leader and protector of the overseas territories. She will have full access to Indonesian oil and Malaysian tin and rubber, and she will have markets for her goods. If necessary she will be backed in securing these by China.

The deal is struck, and the moves are made. There is no aggression at all in the old sense of the word. Japan secures bases: Hong Kong, deserted by the British, becomes a Japanese base. To counter the Soviet bases in Vietnam, Singapore has granted the Americans the old British naval base, and as Japan has taken up the major responsibility for defense of Asia at the American demand, Japan has succeeded to these rights. The Japanese have also moved into Malaysia with a base and into Indonesia, all with the concurrence of the local governments in the name of defense. Where needed, Japan now has bases and treaties to insure them, and her economic presence and security are likewise insured. Japan has the markets she needs and a triangular trade involving the largest group of consumers in the world, the Chinese. It has all been done without the wave of a samurai sword, but behind it is the force of Japan's modern military machine.

The only overt act in the whole drama is the swift, virtually bloodless invasion of Taiwan, the running down of the red-white-and-blue Chinese flag and the running up of the red banner on the Taipei flagpoles. As Beijing has promised, there is scarcely a stir in the economic climate of Taiwan, for the Beijing economic czars know a good thing when they have got one.

Is there anything to stop this move?

Obviously the United Nations is not going to stop it, no matter how many on the sidelines holler "foul." The only war effort that ever involved the UN was the Korean War, and that was a fluke, the ultimate result of which was to return to the status quo ante 1950 with no gain at all for anyone, and the first major loss of prestige by superpower America.

Besides, there is no war here.

Certainly the United States is not at this late date going to be able to stop Japan, for the United States, having set the machine into motion, has paid virtually no attention as the Japanese have moved steadily, quietly toward pursuit of their own interests. In the 1970s the United States began to admit its weaknesses in its demands for Japan to rearm. The enormous burden on Americans has continued, the North Atlantic Treaty Organization has finally collapsed under the weight of European neutralism and the United States has been pushed into a new stance that would be very familiar to a student of defense affairs from the late 1930s.

No, redress will certainly not come from the United States, given the Vietnam syndrome. There is only one war the United States is prepared to wage: that against the Soviet Union. American opinion on Taiwan is divided, as it has been for more than a quarter-century.

Would the Soviet Union stop Japan?

Hardly, given the standoff with the United States, which ties up most of the USSR's military resources. Then, also, there is the long Sino-Soviet border. Besides all that, the USSR has had little love for the Nationalist government since the 1920s, and after that government went to Taiwan, no love at all. In the 1980s, especially following the serious miscalculation in Afghanistan, the USSR, like the United States, developed a distinct wariness toward all but the most essential foreign excursions.

The fact is that by the year 2000 the superpowers have become muscle-bound, competent only to destroy one another, restricted to lesser actions through "client" nations. Even within their own close spheres of influence, as Afghanistan, Poland, Rumania, Cuba, Nicaragua and El Salvador indicated, the superpowers were unable to exercise the sort of controls so common a quarter-century earlier in Hungary, Czechoslovakia, Guatemala and Chile. They are not likely to impose themselves on territorial changes in Southeast Asia.

The scene is impossible? Perhaps. But it happened once before, in the 1930s in Manchuria and China, a different time, a different way. This time, given a minimum of violence, the result is likely to be far more permanent.

What is more than possible in 2001 is that China and Japan, in alliance, become a third superforce of the world, Japan supplying the high technology and China the manpower and national resources.

2
The New Militarists

In 1945, after the Americans occupied Japan and staged the war crimes trials, they set about revolutionizing Japanese society. The Japanese, through newspapers, the airwaves and books were made to understand that theirs was the sole responsibility for the Pacific War. That heavy burden of guilt was emphasized in the new textbooks introduced into the schools. All was being changed. From an imperial power Japan was to be made into a constitutional monarchy, and she was never again to have the power to make war. She was, as General MacArthur put it, to be transformed into "the Switzerland of Asia."

The methods of bringing about this halcyon future invoked a major debate in the winter of 1946. The matter was settled in a meeting between General MacArthur and Prime Minister Kijuro Shidehara. At that moment the question of the future of the emperor was hanging in the balance; many of the victors, including the Soviets and some Americans, felt that the emperor should go on trial as a war criminal. MacArthur was shrewder; he believed that the success or failure of the American occupation rested on the fate of the emperor. If Hirohito were tried and executed he

17

would continue as a god, and ultimately the Japanese would revive the old ways. Prime Minister Shidehara urged that opinion, for reasons of his own. On January 24, 1946, Shidehara proposed that the emperor be absolved from "war guilt" and that in return the Japanese would guarantee in their new constitution to refrain from any military activity in the future.

So it was done, and the result was Article IX of the new Japanese constitution in which the Japanese "forever renounce war as a sovereign right of the nation."

For Japan's protection in the future, she was to rely on the United Nations. Yes, this was said quite seriously in the middle 1940s.

The idealistic staff of the supreme commander for the Allied powers set out to expunge everything military from Japanese life. The old national anthem "Kimigayo" was banned as too military. The Yasukuni Shrine, where the souls of all heroic Japanese soldiers were consigned by the gods, was divested of its heroic stature. The educational system was "reformed" along the American pattern of 6–3–3—six years of elementary school, three years of junior high school, three years of high school. The control of the educational system was taken away from the central government and, again in the American fashion, put into the hands of local school boards.

All possible was done to expunge the respect in which the Japanese held the military. Even judo and similar systems—sometimes called aerobic exercise, sometimes called self-defense—were banned as "martial arts."

As time went on many Japanese came to believe in Article IX—the element of the constitution that denied perpetually the rearmament of Japan. Not all: for example, a young naval officer named Yasuhiro Nakasone was so stricken by the change in Japan's affairs that for years he wore a black tie on the grounds that "every Japanese should be in mourning." In mourning for what was, in the Japanese fashion, not precisely stated, but events of the 1980s, when Nakasone became Japan's prime minister, indicate that Nakasone's mourning was for times past, not for "Japanese guilt."

Attempts were made in 1947, before the new constitution came into effect, to bring about the rearmament of Japan. A Japanese foreign office spokesman called on McMahon Ball, an Australian delegate of the British Commonwealth in Tokyo, to suggest that Japan be rearmed with a hundred-thousand-man force when the Allies withdrew the occupation forces. He also made overtures to E. H. Norman, a Canadian diplomat in Tokyo. At the time nothing came of those proposals, but, as will be seen, Japanese rearmament still began before the Korean War broke out.

Many political leaders, and particularly the Socialists, did take the new constitutional provisions literally. But, within three years Article IX was being subverted. Having changed their minds on the issue almost immediately after forcing the constitution on Japan, the Americans indicated the need for change. When Japanese objected that change was not possible, the Americans noted that amending a constitution was hardly more than a formality. Their own had been amended twenty-one times. Once again, in that contention Americans showed how little they had learned about the nation they had fought, conquered and tried to rebuild in the American image. Those Japanese who had *believed* that they could live in a world without armament had come to realize that the Americans might speak in terms of high morality and idealism but that they acted in pragmatic response to what they saw as their own interests.

The 1960s and 1970s brought new culture shocks to Japan. The result was that in the middle 1980s, while ostensibly joining hands with the Americans in the latter's demand for a united defense (under American leadership) against the USSR, the Japanese decided that their interests were not necessarily those of the United States, and their diplomatic and military posture began to change accordingly. The economic burden forced on Japan during the recession of 1980 by the demands of American business and labor for protection against Japanese competition destroyed much of what was left of Japanese-American amity. By 1984 the Japanese politicians of the right, who had led the country almost constantly for ninety years, began looking once more to Japan's own interests and finding that, as in the 1930s, they lay with those of China.

But China was no longer the sleeping giant that Napoleon had seen. She was the largest nation in the world in terms of population, and except for the nagging absence of Taiwan, which stuck out to the Chinese like the missing piece of a jigsaw puzzle, China was integrated and on the way to completion of "the four modernizations" decreed by the second generation of Chinese leaders since the revolution of 1948. A little behind schedule, China was still within reach of the transformation into a modern economic power through modernization of agriculture, science and technology, industry and defense. But since China's interests lay on the continent of Asia, pragmatically she had been ready to strike a deal with Japan, whose major defense element was the sea.

The Japanese decided in the 1970s that the American shining example established in the 1940s as conquerors was tarnished. The American disaster in Vietnam, followed by the American economic disaster (recession) at home offered Japan a powerful new economic opportunity. These two American problems were accompanied by another: The almost constant state of war in which the United States had found itself since 1950 had artificially propped up its industrial system. With the evacuation of Saigon, for the first time since the French gave up their attempt to control events on the Indo-Chinese peninsula and the Americans decided they could succeed where France had failed, the United States military was basically unoccupied, and the factories that had produced the matériel of war were shutting down their assembly lines. Suddenly the deficiencies of an outmoded war industry system became exposed.

It was not long before the combination of American recession and American distaste for military adventure made itself felt in the enormous Pacific Defense Command established during World War II. The U.S. commander-in-chief of the Pacific was responsible for everything military from San Francisco to the eastern shores of Africa. It was too great a task, and in the 1970s the pressure was put on Japan to take over part of it. The Japanese seemed to resist, but by 1984 they had increased their military budgets several times to become the eighth largest military spender in the world. The Diet (Japanese parliament) had approved expenditures amounting to 1 percent of the national budget. It might seem like a small figure to outsiders, but to Japanese who had been told by their government that it would never again engage in outside military activity, the growth of the military was a shock. By 1984 the Japanese people were being persuaded to accept the new wave of self-defense. They were becoming used to it, but as of 1984 had not been called upon to do anything except increase the size of the force. So the Japanese defense muscle was in no way being flexed. This would come at the point when the Americans gave the Japanese actual control of some element of defense, such as the responsibility for patrolling the Pacific for a thousand miles around the Japanese islands, a complex task urged on Japan in 1983. Once that responsibility was assumed it could not be withdrawn, and the manner of its exercise would be Japanese. If there developed differences of opinion, then the crunch would begin.

What was essential (but not discussed publicly in 1984 so there was no indication of American understanding) was the development of a whole new military and economic partnership. There was no proof in the statements of high American officialdom that they understood what the American changes were doing to Japan or that they—the United States—could show the leadership and forbearance essential to the creation of the new sort of relationship that was necessary.

The Japanese already showed signs of a political awakening to match their new military posture. It was not until the 1970s that Japan and China "regularized" their relations. Regularized is hardly the word—for the first time in history China and Japan, the two most powerful nations in Asia, met as equals. The manner of their address to the meetings in 1983 and 1984 indicated the strong possibility of China and Japan creating a power orbit of their own, particularly if the United States failed to move positively to strengthen its relationships with China. And this did not mean more Coca-Cola or more CBS television network programming

in Shanghai. At some point—and legendary Chinese patience is
not illimitable—America would have to reverse its Taiwan pro-
tective policy or take the consequences. In 1984 there was still no
indication in Washington that this inevitability was really understood—or at least accepted.

Beginning in 1983 the world saw an exchange of visits of high-
level personages between China and Japan. Hu Yao-bang, secretary of the Chinese Communist party, led a delegation to Japan
in November and engaged in talks with Japanese Prime Minister
Yasuhiro Nakasone and various Japanese ministers. They addressed themselves to the matter of peace in Korea, something the
Americans and Soviets had never been able to resolve.

The Chinese expressed their sympathy to the Japanese over the
question of Sakhalin and the other three northern islands taken by
the USSR as the spoils of World War II. The atmosphere was
downright jolly except for a few expressed misgivings. The Chinese
brought up the irritation of continued U.S. support of Taiwanese
independence. They did not exactly blame Japan for this situation
but mentioned it because of the close relationship between Japan
and the United States. Prime Minister Nakasone was discreetly
silent on this matter.

Secretary Hu spoke of the expressed fears of some Asian nations
about the expansion of Japanese military power, and the continued
existence of groups in Japan that advocate a revival of Japanese
militarism. Nakasone was quick to insist that Japan would stick
to its "peace constitution" and "exclusively defensive defense." All
this came at a time when the Japanese had already abandoned both,
and were yielding more rapidly than ever to the push—much of
it ironically from the U.S.—to build a powerful military machine.

Secretary Hu visited Hokkaido, to call attention to the Soviet
occupation of the northern islands. Hu and Nakasone reached a
final agreement pledging friendship through the twenty-first century. This was all heady new stuff in Asia, made meaningful by
the enormous economic power of Japan and the physical power
of China. Another indication of the change was seen in China.
Suddenly Japanese had become the second most popular foreign

language in Chinese schools, the first being English. Some eighteen hundred teachers were employed at Chinese universities teaching Japanese. Some thirty-five thousand Chinese students at sixty universities were taking four-year Japanese courses. Millions of other Chinese were studying Japanese at other levels. The government of China was obviously supporting the change. A group of Japanese journalists touring China in 1984 was surprised to discover the large number of Chinese who spoke Japanese. Tai Kawabata, a reporter for the *Japan Times*, said, "before going to China this writer had expected that Japanese would be totally incommunicable and studied a Chinese phrase book. But there was no need..."

Suddenly, after years of virtual isolation from each other, China and Japan were moving toward some sort of alliance. What sort of alliance is a matter that has worried the other nations of Asia in the 1980s. It was an undercurrent in the meetings of the Association of Southeast Asian Nations (ASEAN) in the summer of 1984. The American secretary of state, George Shultz, and the Japanese foreign minister, Shintaro Abe, were at some pains to emphasize that Japanese and American efforts to woo China would not be at the expense of the other nations of Asia. Those other nations in 1984 were also extremely nervous at the prospect of increased Japanese rearmament. They seemed to realize far better than the U.S. that to every extent that Japan increased her military power, Japan's dependence on the United States was decreased, and the impetus to move out from the "American umbrella" was magnified. The other Asian nations, which once lived under Hakko Ichiu (the eight corners of the world under one roof—a Japanese roof) had not so soon forgotten. Once, a Greater East Asia Co-Prosperity Sphere had proved of immediate value only to Japan, although of long-range value to all the ancient colonies, who through the efforts of the Pacific War shook off their colonial masters. But given wartime Japan's rough treatment of those Asian neighbors at the time, little gratitude could be expected. Now that independence has been the norm for more than thirty years, any reason for gratitude was forgotten. The uncomfortable feeling of

Asians when they considered the prospect of a rearmed Japan, one of the most ferocious fighting nations of history, was not and is not forgotten at all.

In the spring of 1984, Prime Minister Nakasone returned the state visit of the Chinese with his own trip to Beijing. He had pondered the statements of Secretary Hu and now gave some answers, including a promise that China would never again have to worry about Japan:

"Some time ago China raised the question of whether militarism might be revived in Japan," he said. "As the person with the ultimate political responsibility for Japan, I can state here and now, without the slightest hesitation, that our nation will never allow a resurgence of militarism."

This same blanket denial that what once was could ever be again, was also coming out of Washington. Anyone who mentioned the possibility that Japanese militarism might be revived was put down with all the vehemence of which the U.S. bureaucracy is capable. One State Department spokesman in ridiculing the notion said the Japanese now possessed a thoroughly modern—emphasis on the "modern"—military force. His point seemed to be that *bushido*, the driving force of Japanese militarism of the 1920s–1940s, was a *feudal* concept. That much was true only in the narrowest sense. The Japanese militarists of the 1920s had indeed revived the feudal concept of superpatriotism and self-denial for their own purposes. But they, too, in the 1930s and 1940s, had a "modern military establishment," the most modern in Asia. The possibility of a resurgence of militarism was not raised even to deny it; apparently the U.S. government was following the theory that one did not mention the unmentionable. It might be unpatriotic for Americans in the 1980s even to consider such a possibility, but it certainly was high on the list of questions of others in the world, particularly those who had been affected by Japanese militarism in the past. The Chinese were not bashful. It must have been obvious to them that Prime Minister Nakasone's promise could be meaningful only as long as he retained the power he held in 1984, and Nakasone would not retain that power forever. So his promises and the words of Americans pressing Japan for greater military growth deserved careful examination within the framework of the trends in Japanese society to determine whether or not it was "impossible" for militarism to again rear its head as both Japan's Liberal Democratic government and the American government insisted.

The degree of nervousness among Japanese in this matter was indicated by a minor incident that occurred in Nagoya in 1983. A welder named Takashi Iwabashi who was badly in debt and desperate for money was looking around for a way to swindle the mass media out of a chunk of money. What to do? What national worry could he use as capital? It would have to be some concern so basic that the victims would not take their usual care to avoid gulling.

Iwabashi found one. He pretended to be a former staff member of the Japanese Self-Defense Forces, the military agency established by the Japanese in the mutual defense treaty with the United States, signed in 1960 with the pious claim that it would never operate outside Japan. Iwabashi donned an SDF uniform and, thus attired, met with a reporter of the magazine *Shukan Sankei* at a Nagoya hotel and gave him "top secret" information about a plot within the SDF organization to overthrow the Japanese government. The editors of *Shukan Sankei* paid Iwabashi ¥315,000 (about $1,300) for the information. He also met with reporters from the Tokyo *Shimbun* and Nihon TV and let them in on the "plot."

The reporters were ready to believe. Always deep in the Japanese consciousness is the memory of an army and navy machine that rose steadily during the 1930s to control Japanese society and by 1940 had achieved its aim and had no further restraints to forbid its embarking on foreign adventures. Iwabashi's story made an overnight sensation in Japan. It was the subject of an investigation in the Diet, and for a time it was nearly swallowed, because the Japanese know that what happened once could not be dismissed so lightly and in such blanket fashion as the U.S. and Japanese governments in the 1980s were dismissing the possibility of a resurgent Japanese militarism.

Confidence man Iwabashi was arrested, tried, convicted and

sentenced to two years in prison for fraud. But his crime could easily be repeated. The idea of a revived militarism stimulates the underlying gloom of Japanese society. As one concerned Japanese friend of mine put it: "Militarism can never return to Japan... but I am afraid." She was a middle-aged schoolteacher; she had lived as a teenager through the end of the Pacific War. She could remember, and she was afraid.

In the reluctance to discuss militarism per se, it is not really that the government of the United States and the government of Japan are trying to cover up some plot or covert movement in Japanese society. After all, what is there to say, what is there to cover up? The two governments are accurate in stating that the U.S. and Japan are operating on essentially a cooperative basis, that Japan is taking a greater share of the responsibility for the Western world's Pacific defenses against the USSR. But no Japanese prime minister or American president or secretary of state can say with a ring of absolute truth that they customarily use that this tenuous condition will stay static. Here is an American State Department brief (called Gist) on Japanese-American security relationships as of October 1983:

> Although an assertive military role in international relations is precluded by its constitution and government policy, Japan's cooperation with the U.S. through the 1960 bilateral Treaty of Mutual Cooperation and Security has been crucial in maintaining peace and stability in East Asia. The bases and facilities in Japan provided under the treaty enable the U.S. to maintain its commitments to other allies in the region, as well as Japan. Japan has significantly strengthened its *self-defense* [italics, author's] capabilities.... This will also allow us more flexibility in responding to emergencies in the southwest Pacific and Indian oceans.

The American position here means to put Japan in a subordinate or junior-partner role, implying that decisions about what "emergencies" need response be left to the U.S. But as Japan continues to renew her military capability, once one of the greatest in the world, and given her enormous economic growth and *bushido* heritage, how long will her leaders be prepared to accept such a role? How long will they be allowed to by the Japanese people?

And what if Japan should suddenly gibe at some American decision? The scene depicted at the beginning of this book does not then seem quite so remote with a powerfully armed Japan as it did with the Japan of the 1960s, when the war machine existed only in the television monster movies for which Tokyo became world-famous.

Of course, there is the matter of nomenclature. Militarism will come in a new guise. The old militarism was characterized by Japanese as *gunkokushugi*, using the four characters that signify "army," "country," "master" and "justice" equaling national military rule. In the manner of the times, a resurgent militarism in Japan will, in the fashion of the U.S. and Soviets, be designated by a new, self-serving phrase that speaks only of "defense."

But defense against what? Against whom? Can we be so sure the answer is, will always be, the Soviets and their client states? Does Japan's economic warfare of late with the U.S. signal nothing? Does it have no possible military analogue? Have we forgotten history so soon—the history of Japan itself, and of its behavior in the years preceding Pearl Harbor?

Safe to say, the American proconsul of Japan after its surrender in 1945, Douglas MacArthur, and his chief, President Harry S. Truman, would have been together in their astonishment at the U.S. State Department's rosy view of Japan's resurgent militarism. Could our memories, they might well have asked, really be so short?

3

The Disarmament That Didn't

Japan will be completely disarmed and demilitarized. The authority of the Militarists and the influence of militarism will be totally eliminated from her political, economic and social life. Institutions expressive of the spirit of militarism and aggression will be vigorously suppressed....

> —Directive by President Harry S. Truman to General Douglas MacArthur, August, 1945

Japan, said the president of the United States, was to have no army, navy, air force, secret police or even civil aviation. All military and naval matériel, vessels, aircraft and installations were to be disposed of by General MacArthur.

After the surrender, Japan's seven remaining aircraft carriers were scrapped, as were three battleships, twelve cruisers, and three auxiliary ships. The remaining submarine force, including midget submarines, was destroyed. Japan's aircraft were destroyed. This work was carried out so thoroughly that at the end not a single Mitsubishi type-0 bomber (Betty) remained; this two–engine bomber had been the workhorse of the Japanese naval forces. The same treatment was accorded army matériel and installations. Only those bases in Japan that could be used by the Americans were retained. The others were ordered to be destroyed.

The destruction and demobilization of the ten-million-man Japanese army and navy were carried out by Japanese organizations.

The War Ministry was dissolved, but a number of officers were retained in the First Demobilization Ministry.

The Japanese army officers did not go without a struggle. Colonel Takushiro Hattori, a member of the Imperial General Staff, drew up a plan for an army of fifteen divisions that could be expanded to fifty divisions in time of war. But the government section of SCAP (Supreme Command, Allied Powers) would not allow any such plan. The three hundred thousand officers of the Japanese army officers' corps were demobilized, although some of them found employment in various police and public safety agencies. The Japanese army personnel officers, however, kept careful records of the demobilization, as well as of the whereabouts of many of those officers who had been sent out to pasture. They took, it would seem, a long view.

The Ministry of the Navy was converted to the Second Demobilization Ministry. The officials retained were vetted by SCAP in the interest of securing "moderates" free of suspicious background that might be construed as "militarist" and with no connection with any "war crimes."

Nationalistic organizations, of which there were many in Japan, were all banned. One of every four teachers was purged, about one hundred twenty thousand in all. The big economic combines (*zaibatsu*) were ordered broken up.

The Allies set up an international tribunal "to mete out stern justice to all war criminals." The British objected that the Allies ought to execute the Japanese leaders and have done with it but the Americans insisted on clothing the proceedings in a legality termed "international." Starting in January, 1946, two thousand Japanese were banned from public life as irredeemable but not quite war criminals. Another five thousand military and civilian officials were tried and given prison terms of various lengths for "war crimes," and General Hideki Tojo, the prime minister who took Japan into the war and remained in power until after the fall of Saipan, was found personally responsible for committing crimes against peace and was hanged. So were a number of others, ranging from General Iwane Matsui, who presided over the rape of Nanking, to former Prime Minister Koki Hirota, who was convicted as civilian "front man" for the army. The Japanese regarded the proceedings as the vengeance of the victors on the vanquished. The larger moral purpose was lost on the Japanese. As the years passed it became apparent that what the Americans had done was establish a new method of eliminating the enemy's leaders, satisfactory to the moral standards of the victors but promising a variety of complications for the future.

The purge-restrictions of SCAP also took away many of the civil rights of military officers. The purges were designed to stamp out the military and naval castes and prevent their future resurgence. But can one generation control another? Particularly when the army and navy could not be demobilized without demobilizers, and so certain officers were exempted from the purge, officers who set out to follow the Allies' will.

The destruction of oceangoing vessels, begun enthusiastically by the Allied naval and air forces and completed by the occupying powers and the vanquished Japanese, left Japan with so little shipping that most of the six million Japanese soldiers and sailors stranded abroad had to be brought home in Allied vessels. About a sixth of them, in Chinese and Soviet territory, were held captive, some for years, and as of the 1980s many had never again been heard from.

By 1947 in the United States it was generally believed that Japan had been disarmed and had accepted the idea of disarmament for all time as the new Japanese constitution indicated.

The fact was, though, that Japan was never totally disarmed. Nor was there ever a consensus about this among the Japanese politicians and military leaders. True, as noted, Prime Minister Shidehara had traded the "renunciation of force" for the life of the emperor. The emperor, at the time he had forced the surrender, had told his people that they must bear the unbearable; and he proceeded to lead. Ordered by SCAP, Hirohito publicly renounced his divinity on January 1, 1946, and adopted a program that was to prove that he was no more than a man, after all. He appeared several times in public, which had not happened before. He took his wife to a baseball game, where they sat in seats like mortals. When the draft constitution which declared him to be only a symbol of the state was prepared, he approved it.

But when the constitution was submitted to the Japanese government in February, 1946, many ministers balked. The new constitution created "people's sovereignty" with the emperor reduced to a symbol as constitutional monarch, the establishment of a new Diet with political parties, and guarantees of individual liberties and rights, including women's suffrage. The constitution created an American-style government, with separation of executive, legislative and judicial functions in a completely non-Japanese fashion.

Kichisaburo Nomura, one of the privy councillors, objected strenuously to Article IX, the outlawry of militarism. He asked what would happen if China, Korea or the Philippines ever attacked Japan. Submission to the Potsdam Declaration required disarmament, he said, but not perennial renunciation of armament. "Even absolutely neutral countries like Switzerland have military forces, and *against Korea we will need armament of some kind.*" (Italics, author's.)

But nothing came of such objections at the time because the draft constitution had already been shown to the emperor and he had accepted the principles. To the Americans the emperor's renunciation of his divinity was meaningful, but to the Japanese the emperor's word was still a command from on high. Shidehara never told his ministers that he had made the renunciation suggestion, and since it purportedly came from the conquerors the Japanese accepted it only reluctantly.

The best that could be done by the objecting ministers was some fiddling with the wording—meaningful only to the Japanese—as showing that Japan independently desired international peace and expected other countries to behave in the same manner.

And so came into being Article IX of the new, or MacArthur, Japanese constitution:

> Aspiring sincerely to an international peace based on justice
> and order, the Japanese people forever renounce war as a sov-

ereign right of the nation and the threat or use of force as a
means of settling international disputes.

In order to accomplish the aim of the preceding paragraph,
land, sea, and air forces, as well as other war potential, will
never be maintained. The right of belligerency of the state will
not be recognized.

The first postwar Japanese election was held in April, 1946. The
Minseito and Seiyukai parties won the most seats and both were
tied to members of the *zaibatsu,* the old clique of industrialists that
had financed the war. Minseito was closely associated with the
Mitsubishis, Seiyukai was associated with the Mitsuis; the *zaibatsu,*
which was supposed to be broken up now, was clearly still very
much a political factor. Shigeru Yoshida, a protégé of Baron Tanaka, who had been condemned as a militarist, became prime minister. He had to be acceptable to the Americans, because in the
last days of the war he had been thrown into jail by the army
leaders for advocating surrender. Who could gainsay that?

In 1947 the Socialist party won the largest bloc of votes and
managed to organize a government—the Socialists were more
attuned to the announced aims of the occupation than any other
element in Japan. Tetsu Katayama became the prime minister. But
the Socialist victory worried General MacArthur, and with the
falling apart of the Nationalist government of China, General
MacArthur decided that Japan must become the American bulwark
in the Far East. He began to reverse SCAP policies. The victory
of the Socialists had also alarmed many Americans at home, so
various policies changed; the breakup of the *zaibatsu* was slowed
down and decentralization of power was stopped. The land reform
program, forced by the Americans, created a new middle class of
landed farmers (87 percent of the land owned by resident farmers)
and their politics became more conservative.

Not surprisingly the Socialist government lasted only six months.
It was succeeded by a coalition government under Hitoshi Ashida.
It, too, survived only six months. Then Yoshida's conservative
government returned to power after the elections of 1949 and

remained until the end of the American occupation.

Throughout all these changes the Japanese military was still hard at work. The initial public safety problem to be solved in 1945 was the elimination of about a hundred thousand mines sowed by the Japanese and the Allies in the waters around Japan. Obviously for the interests of all concerned these had to be removed. When the first Japanese contingent to discuss the surrender terms had flown to Manila in August, 1945, it had been agreed that the minesweeping would begin, and from that time until September the Japanese worked at it. Sweeping operations were discontinued, though, while the Americans worked out their occupation plans. An enormous pressure was building in America to "bring the boys home." The result was that minesweeping was left entirely in Japanese hands under "the Second Demobilization Ministry," which was the new occupation name for the Imperial Japanese Navy. By May, 1946, all American minesweepers had left Japan. The theoretically demobilized Japanese navy was hard at work polishing wartime skills. The officers and men were stripped of the visible evidence of rank, but otherwise operated as of old; for example: Captain Kyozo Tamura, in charge of minesweeping, was not Captain Tamura anymore but Coastal Security Senior Officer First Class Tamura. The Americans estimated that all the minesweeping would be completed by 1947. Actually it was not finished until some twenty-five years later in the 1970s.

The rather simplistic nature of the American program for Japan was indicated in still another way. The end of the war left Japan without any means of protecting its harbors or sea lanes. Japanese fishermen who went to sea in their boats were quite likely to be captured by Koreans, Chinese or Russians, who wanted those boats. The Japanese complained to the occupation forces, and were stalled. But in the summer of 1946 a cholera outbreak in Korea brought the matter to a head. Koreans began moving across the Korea Strait to Japan by the thousands. The officials of SCAP finally established the Japanese Maritime Safety Agency to deal with the problems of illegal entry and smuggling. Twenty-eight former navy patrol boats were saved from scrapping and turned over to the new agency, which became part of the Ministry of Transportation. So now Japan had a "coast guard," and an American Coast Guard officer, Captain Frank M. Meals, worked out the details of organization with the Japanese. The Maritime Safety Agency, he said, was not a military force any more than the U.S. Coast Guard was a military force. What he did not say was that it was not any less of one either, and during World War II the military nature of the U.S. Coast Guard was clearly demonstrated when it was transferred lock, stock and barrel to the navy for the duration of the war with virtually no difficulty, administrative or operational.

The true problem, though, was not that *some* military force needed to be retained in Japan, but that the myth of total Japanese disarmament had to be maintained or it was totally destroyed. If Japan was truly to be disarmed, then the United States would have to assume all the legitimate functions of the military, but the U.S. Congress and the navy were not willing to provide the necessary forces to police Japanese home waters. Had they tried, quite probably they would have failed—simply because they had so little knowledge of the area. In retrospect, the decision to form the Japanese agency seems rather sensible. The trouble was that the international political situation of the day made it necessary to disguise the reality and create a myth that became ever weightier. Not only Americans began to believe the myth, the Japanese people did too. And this played into the hands of the Japanese Socialist party, which came out of the war era with considerable following. The Socialists opposed war as a matter of principle, so Article IX of the constitution became an internal political matter of great importance. A peace party, after all, rouses the opposition.

Article IX was important in another way. Japanese military men, as mentioned, had learned almost immediately that there were ways to avoid the final dissolution of the Japanese military and naval systems, and the Americans learned that on an operational level certain accommodations had to be made. How to continue to sweep away the mines that had been planted in the coastal waters

of Japan? Transfer the job to the new benign-sounding Maritime
Safety Agency. Takeo Okuba, its head, controlled 350 ships, 773
officers and 9,227 enlisted men! Rear Admiral Yoshio Yamamoto,
who had been supervising the demobilization of the Japanese navy,
came aboard as senior military officer. Coastal Security Senior
Officer First Class Tamura was now reappointed captain in this
new force to supervise the minesweeping. So in 1947, less than
two years after their surrender, the Japanese had a real naval force
again, with no limit on the number of ships, armament or speed.
It was, of course, called a "nonmilitary agency."

In April, 1948, the Japanese government under Prime Minister
Hitoshi Ashida would put through the Diet a new law enlarging
the concept with the establishment of a Maritime Safety Board.
This agency would have a total of 10,000 personnel and 125 vessels.
Soviet representatives at Supreme Headquarters charged that the
Japanese navy had just been reborn. The American response was
that all of the vessels were slow (15 knots) and a threat to no one.
This was truer than anyone liked to believe at the time: Smugglers,
whose armament had no political overtones, often had faster vessels and better armament than the Japanese safety forces. But the
structure, regardless of vessel-speed, was still there.

During the summer of 1948 the Japanese government changed.
Socialist leader Tetsu Katayama became prime minister while Hitoshi Ashida moved over to become foreign minister. Ashida prepared a policy statement enunciating a new military idea: Japan
would provide for her own security against minor attack, would
rely on the United States for protection against major attack. And
so was born the first postwar military defense policy, in a nation
that had foresworn it.

Meanwhile the Japanese military men were not nearly so supine
as appeared on the surface. A number of senior officers met secretly
and decided to make of the Documents Division of the Second
Demobilization Ministry (old Navy Ministry) "a core for carrying
out confidential studies..." Captain Eizo Yoshida, chief of the
Documents Division, worked secretly at night and in spare time

with Captain Masataka Nagaishi and Commander Yoshimori Terai. Throughout a number of changes in the organization of the naval demobilization system, Captain Yoshida retained office and continued his secret work. By the summer of 1948 the Japanese government had transferred the liquidation of the navy to the Welfare Ministry, and Captain Yoshida was head of the Material Liquidation Section of the Repatriation Relief Agency within that ministry—a comfortable place for clandestine naval-rearmament planning.

All this while Captain Yoshida was consulting with Admiral Yamamoto, chief operating officer of the nonmilitary Maritime Safety Agency and Captain Ko Nagasawa, formerly of the Imperial Japanese Navy's bureau of personnel, who kept the records of officer demobilization and kept track of the officers afterward. The Japanese navy had been disbanded, but a cadre within the official government family knew where they were and how to bring them back, when the time came.

A number of retired Japanese naval men supported the planning and gave advice, the most important of whom was Admiral Kichisaburo Nomura, who had been one of the Japanese negotiators in Washington at the time of the Pearl Harbor attack.

This activity was also carried out with the benign approval of a number of active and retired American naval officers, who recognized, as American politicians did not, that a maritime nation would never believe it could exist independently without a naval force of some sort. Such as Rear Admiral D. W. Beary could not admit publicly their views, nor could Beary, as naval representative of SCAP, give any official endorsement to such activity.

But by November, 1948, some of the unanticipated consequences of the unconditional surrender and war crimes trials imposed on the defeated enemies were becoming apparent to official Washington. Indeed, that month the U.S. National Security Council recommended the encouragement of "paramilitary activity" in Japan.

Nothing much more came of this change in attitude until the summer of 1950 when, late in June, the North Korean army marched without warning across the thirty-eighth parallel into South Korea and the Korean War began. The immediate reaction in Tokyo was that a "police action" by one or two American divisions should be able to solve the problem, but the divisions did have to be moved out of Japan and to Korea. Available American naval units also had to move into battle. That action, in turn, had to leave a vacuum in the occupation force, and on July 8, General MacArthur wrote Prime Minister Yoshida asking him to establish a National Police Reserve. It was done. The moving factor was Lieutenant General Eiichi Tatsumi. Prime Minister Yoshida, who had been jailed during the war by the militarist government of Japan, had little use for the old militarists, and was not pleased with the idea of bringing army officers back into public service, but General Tatsumi argued that the Americans were pulling out and that Japan had to have a force of its own and it had to be effective. So in 1950 the colonels came back into military service and the way was set for reestablishment of the old tradition. Also, pursuant to another request by General MacArthur, the Diet approved an increase in the size of the Maritime Safety Board force by eight thousand men.

At this time Rear Admiral Arleigh Burke, who was Admiral Turner Joy's number two man in the American naval force in Japan, suggested that Japan had to have a real navy. He suggested that Admiral Nomura find ten of the best officers of the old Imperial Navy and form a new one. It so happened that through Captain Yoshida's secret studies, the Japanese were ready. Almost as if by magic they produced detailed plans which admirals Burke and Joy forwarded to Admiral Forrest Sherman, the U.S. navy's chief-of-staff in Washington.

Meanwhile the American involvement in Korea became far more serious than anyone in Washington or Tokyo had imagined it would be. The first American division sent to Korea (the Twenty-fourth Infantry Division) was slashed to bits by the fast-moving North Koreans. The Twenty-fifth Division and the First Cavalry Division were rushed into the line. Still the North Koreans ground their way steadily south until they reached a line bounded roughly by the Naktong and Nam rivers, a semicircle about fifty miles north of Pusan. There, in August, the Americans and the badly demoralized South Korean forces were finally able to hold. But all the American and Allied forces that could be rushed to Korea had to be used. So the pressure was on the Japanese, no matter how they felt about rearmament, to in fact speed up the process. General MacArthur by this time was thoroughly preoccupied with the Korean War. Then came Prime Minister Yoshida, no friend of the militarists, who ironically was forced by circumstance to employ officers of the old imperial forces because there simply were no others.

With the Inchon landings and the movement of United Nations forces north again, a new problem developed. The North Koreans had little naval power but they did have mines and they used them very effectively. A number of Allied vessels were sunk or damaged. Admirals Joy and Burke saw the need for minesweeping forces, but there were only a handful of American minesweepers available. So in October, 1950, the Japanese sea forces went to war again, and proved themselves much more adept at minesweeping than the Americans. Why not? They had been doing it steadily for five years while the American minesweepers had been put in mothballs, minesweeper officers and men had been sent back to private life and the U.S. navy had virtually forgotten there was such a specialty as antimine warfare. The crisis lasted only a few weeks, then the Japanese minesweepers were detached one by one and returned to their job of sweeping old mines around Japan. But the principle had been established, and one Japanese sailor had been killed and eight injured in *military* activity.

So by 1951 Prime Minister Yoshida had accepted the need for rearmament, no matter what the constitution said. In August, twelve thousand former professional army and navy officers were "depurged" by the Japanese government with the approval of the American occupying forces. President Truman, who had spoken in 1945 of eliminating the authority and influence of the militarists in Japanese society, offered Japan frigates and fifty large landing ships for the new naval organization. The Americans were now talking about training the Japanese military to become "a member of the United Nations team." Under the Marine Safety Agency a new Coastal Security Force was established, and this was the real nucleus of the new Japanese navy. Admiral Yamamoto was asked to head this new force. He asked just what did the prime minister have in mind? Was it to be a navy or a coast guard? If it was the latter Yamamoto was not interested. The chief cabinet secretary told him it would be navy, and he took the job.

And so it had come to pass that those who had secretly drawn up the plans were now selected to run the new Japanese navy. Captain Yoshida, Captain Nagasawa, Captain Terai all moved over from the Second Demobilization Liquidation Bureau, joined by Rear Admiral Jitsue Akishige and a captain who had been purged from the navy earlier in the Allied drive to wipe out militarism.

Temporarily, for political reasons, the new navy had to be concealed under the Marine Safety Agency in the Transportation Ministry, but neither Americans on the advisory committee nor the Japanese of the new navy were under any illusions about the real source of authority. The Marine Safety Agency proposed to take over the fifty landing ships and frigates and distribute them among the ten agency districts around Japan. The navy men said no, the Americans backed them up. And planner Yoshida was ready with a plan—the Coastal Security Force was ready to drop the mantle of the MSA at any moment and take over as the new navy. A clever table of organization was established that showed the Marine Safety Force in charge of everything and the real navy down at the bottom. But the key to it all was that the real navy was down there as a single unit, with the knowledge that at any time it could pull away from the other agency. There, in its cozy unit-designation, was security.

The Japanese planners and their American friends agreed that the Coastal Security Force would consist of six thousand officers and men. Training began under American instructors. It was all started very quietly aboard one of the frigates in Yokosuka harbor on January 19, 1952. In August the split was made and approved by the Diet. The new navy came into being as the Maritime Safety Force, and the new army came into being as the other half of the National Safety Agency. At the same time the Americans and the Japanese government were working out the U.S.–Japanese peace treaty. The exigencies of the Korean War had brought a volte-face by the United States government, and the pattern for Japanese rearmament had been established. It was apparent in the planning of Captain Yoshida and his associates from the beginning that they looked to the day when Japanese interests could be considered for their own sake and not as subsidiary to the Americans.

From 1945 on, slowly, steadily, the Japanese military moved toward that end.

1 | War and peace. A World War II anti-
aircraft gun before the museum of the
Yasukuni Shrine, Tokyo. Inside are honored the 2.5 million Japanese war dead.

2 | Naval cadets on parade at their Eta Jima officers' candidate school.

3

4

5

3 | The cadet corps of the Eta Jima academy marches down to the pier to see off comrades on their summer cruise.

4 | Three Tokyo street urchins and the memorial erected in a Tokyo park to General Tojo and five other "war criminals" hanged by the allies.

5 | The administration building of the Eta Jima Self-Defense Force Maritime officers' candidate school.

6 | Athletes all. Officer candidates at the Eta Jima academy run against their own time to improve their speed.

7 | Both men and women join the Japanese Maritime Defense Force.

8 | Kendo (Japanese fencing). Both men and women train in this ancient sport of Japan.

9 | It takes a skilled eye and good reflexes to escape a Kendo bout without bruises.

4

A Fertile Field for Militarism

In the last half of the twentieth century the Japanese were not a happy people. Their world had been turned upside down three times in fifty years. They had been led in the 1930s to believe that Japan would be first among the nations of Asia and of the world. The natural superiority of Japanese civilization, said the militarists who had taken over the government, would at last be understood and all the world would come under the eight corners of their roof. They had already taken Taiwan, Korea and Manchuria. They attacked China, and expected to conquer it. They moved into Indochina and then Malaya, the Dutch East Indies, the Philippines and as far south as New Guinea. They threatened Australia and had plans to invade it. The Kwantung Army firmly expected to attack the Soviet Union and chew off at least Siberia if not more. Dreamers on the general staff foresaw a march across India to the Caucasus, linking up with that other superpower, Germany, and then dominating not only Europe and Asia but the Middle East as well. They would move across the Pacific, taking Hawaii and the Aleutians, and perhaps invading Alaska and even the west coast of the United States.

The militarists had miscalculated, forgetting about the industrial might of the United States, and mistaking Western indolence for cowardice. Instead of conquering the world, Japan lost itself. Its empire disappeared, national pride was trampled, twenty-eight political and military leaders were tried in highly publicized proceedings and seven were hanged. During 1946 and 1947 several thousand Japanese who had participated in capital crimes against civilians and allied military personnel were convicted and executed.

After the 1952 peace treaty with the U.S. came into force a general amnesty by the Japanese government restored civil rights, but the Japanese saw the war-crimes trials as having nothing to do with morality, everything to do with the retribution to the victor. It was not forgotten. Despite the efforts of the Americans to expunge the memory of those executed, a secret monument was erected to the honor of General Tojo and the rest in Higashi-Ikebukuro Park in Tokyo. After American power was removed, thousands came to visit it and meditate on the cost of *losing* a war. They still do, although today the park and its monument sit in the shadow of a great modern skyscraper, the Sun Center. The park is an oasis for office-dwellers, many of them American, most of whom do not know that on the far side of a great boulder at the end of the park is an inscription to Tojo and the other five "criminals." The bare patches of ground off the walkway on the far side show where thousands have stepped back to point their cameras at the inscription.

The Japanese are good followers, and often outstrip their leaders. When their government imposed the new constitution the people in effect accepted it. The military, which had been highly honored since the feudal days of Japan, fell, at least officially, into disrepute. There was no military, by law. The members of Japan's Self-Defense Forces were declared to be civilians. Recruiting for the Self-Defense Forces was, in fact, an enormous problem in the beginning since war was outlawed and perhaps more important the majority of Japanese were turning their minds to business, secure in the new pacifism.

That attitude was fostered by Prime Minister Shigeru Yoshida, who was a hangover from the old days, a prominent member of the foreign office. Late in the 1950s other politicians challenged Yoshida, politicians tired of American dominance and for whom Yoshida represented subservience to the Americans. Ichiro Hatoyama led a group of conservatives that wanted to scrap Article IX of the constitution and rearm, pass strong labor control legislation to stop the rise of the left wing and centralize the police power. The result of Hatoyama's revolutionary plans was a new massing of right and left, with the Liberal Democratic party espousing the Hatoyama position and the leftists moving close around the Japan Socialist party. When in 1957 the conservatives were all for dropping Article IX of the constitution and really rearming, the communists and socialists controlled about a third of the seats in parliament so it could not be done. Hatoyama as prime minister did his best but failed to change the constitution. But the climate *was* changing.

In 1957 Nobosuke Kishi succeeded Hatoyama. His major aim was to wipe out the dependence of Japan on the United States, largely through revision of the Japan–United States security treaty. Again the issue was reduced to pacifism versus rearmament, and in 1960 the uproar was so great that four million people came out to demonstrate against the government and the new mutual defense treaty. President Dwight D. Eisenhower was about to make a "goodwill" trip to Japan. The Kishi government politely asked him not to come, and when the Americans apparently failed to understand what was happening, Kishi let it be known that if Eisenhower did come and there was violence, Kishi would commit suicide. Ultimately Eisenhower did not come. The revised treaty was passed, but the opposition continued to grumble and claim that the treaty violated the constitution, a claim still not abandoned in the 1980s.

The Liberal Democratic party now avoided the conflict over

increased defense and turned all efforts toward economic success, and *that* success story is already legendary. The consensus in Japan was "growthmanship," total commitment to pursuit of the yen. The Japanese were pleased not to have to worry about international politics. Americans would take care of defense.

In the 1960s America began to call for help, first in arming for the Vietnam War, then for aid in the policing of the western Pacific. The Japanese responded tentatively. In 1955 the Japanese had been spending about 2 percent of their gross national product on their own defense efforts. The ratio fell steadily until 1970 when it reached .8 percent. In the 1970s the American call was more strident. And two other factors came into play: The United States was seen to be bogging down in Vietnam in a war so much like the "China incident" that the Japanese could see no difference. Since the end of World War II Japan had been accused of aggression against China. What was America doing against Vietnam? If the Japanese war against China could not be justified, then how could the American action in Vietnam? The internal American conflict between hawks and doves that split the United States so desperately was watched from Tokyo first with disbelief, then with a growing skepticism about the aims of the United States and its ability to carry them out. The Japanese warm placidity under the American umbrella suddenly received a chill. It received another when in 1971 without a word to the Japanese, who were supposed to be America's prime allies in the Pacific, President Nixon sent Henry Kissinger to China to arrange for a presidential visit and made overtures to normalize relations. In Japan this was called the "Nixon Shock," and it stirred the nation.

Although the consensus persisted favoring the peace constitution and its nurturing effect on the growth economy, the military men began a little pushing. In 1968 General Hiromi Kurisu raised a question that had been troubling the Japanese Self-Defense Forces for a long time: How could a military force concern itself totally with "defense"? The SDF, he said, had to have offensive capability. The notion, of course, ran straight up against the pacifist theories, and in the furor over it General Kurisu was fired. The issue had been raised, however, and it would not go away. That same year the politician Yasuhiru Nakasone spoke at Tokyo University advocating the repeal of the antiwar Article IX of the constitution. A few years earlier such talk from a politician had brought student riots. Nakasone was cheered.

When the U.S. in 1972 gave Okinawa back to Japan, the Japanese insisted that the Three Principles of Nuclear Disarmament be observed. This doctrine held that Japan would not possess, manufacture or introduce atomic weapons. In the revised security treaty of 1960 it had been understood that the U.S. would not bring atomic weapons to Japan at all without consultation with the Japanese government, and in 1972 this was extended to Okinawa. But the U.S. almost immediately began violating the agreement, and the Japanese government looked the other way. In 1971, with American urging, the buried hopes of the Liberal Democratic party (LDP) for a revived Japanese military power were tentatively brought forward, and the long process of repositioning the public mind was ready to begin.

More important, though, than American influence was a new Japanese realization. The "Nixon Shock" over the China venture, the sudden withdrawal of America from Vietnam in 1975, the recognition of the Beijing government, the downgrading of the American relationship with Taiwan, President Jimmy Carter's talk of a total military withdrawal from Korea (the "Korea Shock") all indicated that America's thirty-year-old Asia policy had collapsed.

For the first time the notion that Japan might have to defend itself became a matter for serious if still tentative discussion. The LDP was able to begin an increase in defense spending, in spite of Article IX of the constitution. It seemed that the United States could not be trusted. And if the United States could not be trusted, then Japan must find a way to guarantee its own future, or so went the reasoning.

By 1978 Japan had accepted the major changes that had occurred in the Japanese relationship with the United States. The process of finding a new consensus on defense had already begun. In a poll taken in 1978 the question was raised again about dropping Article IX of the constitution and openly rearming; 71 percent of the Japanese polled said they were against the idea, 15 percent favored it, and 14 percent did not know. As for the Japan–U.S. security treaty, less than half thought it served Japan's interests, and, perhaps most significantly, 25 percent were sure it did not.

That lack of confidence went deep:

The question:

When worse comes to worst, do you think the United States will seriously defend Japan?

The answer:

No	56 percent
Yes	20 percent
Confused	24 percent

Even more telling was another question:

What do you think is the most important factor that safeguards Japan?

The answer:

U.S. support	2 percent
Peace diplomacy	42 percent
Economic power	20 percent
Peace constitution	15 percent
Patriotism	13 percent
Self Defense Force	2 percent
Confused	6 percent

Twenty years earlier the Japanese had confidently expected that the Americans would defend them. Their peace constitution would prevent them from harm. The Self-Defense Forces would serve to stop any minor trouble. In 1978 the Japanese no longer believed these things. The first step had been taken to avoid the unacceptable, a vacuum that would be left by American desertion of Japan in time of need, *which the Japanese people now expected.*

Japan was thrown off-balance. Previously when the Japanese were asked which country was their best friend, the response had been overwhelmingly that it was the United States. In 1978, not so.

The question:

With which country do you think Japan should maintain the most friendly relations in the future?

The answer:

The United States	29 percent
China	23 percent
The USSR	3 percent
Confused	45 percent

Nearly half those polled did not know what to do. The United States had destroyed its special position with Japan. The one logical alternative to a strong alliance with the United States, given Japan's military weakness, was Pan-Asianism (note that nearly as many put their hopes in China as in the U.S.). This, of course, was the policy of the old militarist Japan, given up with the defeat in the Pacific War and the demise of the Greater East Asia Co-Prosperity Sphere. Now it once again raised its head. Initial reaction elsewhere in Asia was mixed—memories of the old Japan were not that short. But Japan nonetheless began making tentative gestures to other Asian nations that surpassed the usual search for trade and profit that had marked her recent years. "Foreign aid" as a means of making friends became a definite part of the Japanese program, and many Japanese talked of the need for a Pacific Basin combination.

What was the Japanese role in the world to be? Until the 1970s the Japanese had seen it largely as a continuation of the profitable peace democracy, where Japan had the best of all possible worlds, much protection and little responsibility. That had died. Three ideas presented themselves:

1. A new Japanese-American relationship, with Japan becoming

a more equal power in every way, particularly in the decision-making process. In the autumn of 1984 the United States-Japan Advisory Commission suggested that the United States and Japan merge their military forces and collaborate on military research and development. The idea read well in the report, but in fact it would mean that both nations would give up their military sovereignty. That would mean no serious military action could be taken by either side without consultation with the other. It seemed most unlikely that the United States would be willing to go that far; surely nothing had been done to prepare the American people for such a move, although as the fifteen-member Japanese-American commission realized, it was the logical step if the Japanese-American alliance was to withstand the tests of time. The alliance in the 1980s was beginning to shudder visibly because of the military and economic demands made on Japan by the United States. The logical development would be a strong Pacific Community in which China also played a large role, but again, the Americans were not prepared for a commonwealth. Such, however, was Prime Minister Nakasone's vision. In December, 1984, he proposed that the United States and Japan move toward creation of a Pacific Basin Community, including southeastern Asian nations and China. It was a central part of Nakasone's agenda. The meeting between Nakasone and President Reagan in the early days of 1985 was a mutual recognition of concern over the new fragility of the political and military alliance in view of the economic pressures. But a true partnership was something the U.S. had never undertaken except in time of war; even NATO had gone only halfway.

2. A pacifist Japan that would rely on diplomacy to protect itself. To achieve this it would have to dissolve the political and military ties to the United States, substituting closer ties with China *and* the USSR. This was the program advocated by Japan's leftists. If the Socialists ever managed to get back into power, this was the direction in which they would move.

3. A powerful Japan, already the third economic power in the world, building a defense that would protect her from all comers,

and would include nuclear weapons in close conjunction with China and other friendly elements of Asia. The two superpowers thereby would be kept at bay on the edges of the Pacific.

Although Japanese political leaders became aware of this looming shadow in the late 1970s, the American people and media were not made aware of it in the early 1980s. The American concern has been limited to its own global policies and the role the American military perceive for Japan. By 1980, with the American recession in full cry, Japan's economic penetration of the U.S. markets for autos, cameras, and electronics peeved a large segment of the business and industrial community of the United States and created the Japan-bashing philosophy, which to the Japanese had some of the overtones of the old Western racism. The Americans seemed unaware that the Japanese harbored a number of resentments out of the past. Americans also did not seem to remember that beginning in 1971 the Japanese had voluntarily restricted their textile exports to the U.S. in recognition of American business complaints (they had then, in fact, found a better market in China). They had made one concession after another to the Americans in matters of trade, particularly in agriculture.

Along with the mutual dissatisfaction over trading relationships, the matter of defense had grown more painful each year, with the U.S. continually asking for more.

And combined resentments and guilt over the war have never gone away. In a heated exchange with a communist leader in 1969 LDP leader Kakuei Tanaka gave an indication of conservative Japan's real feelings about the Pacific War. The talk was about Japan's responsibility for the start of World War II. Tanaka:

"... At that time we Japanese had virtually no natural resources. There were some hundred million of us then, and when we tried to obtain cheap imports we were kicked around by high tariffs. We tried to immigrate elsewhere and were slapped with exclusion. Our export goods were discriminated against. Didn't we hit the very bottom in the Depression? . . ."

As the Pacific War receded and the Japanese saw that the United States in Vietnam lost an aggressive war, America's moral position about the Pacific War tended in Japanese eyes to be eroded. The Japanese were inclined, as Tetsuya Kataoka put it in his study of Japanese defense measures, to see in "America's bungling and subsequent humiliation ... a comeuppance. The way some conservative Japanese cheered on the Vietcong after the 'Nixon Shock' suggests that the Vietcong had become their proxy against white men—even though they knew full well that that was an illusion ... "

In the 1980s the demands of the United States on Japan have become far more open and urgent than ever before. Still, the Japanese people have not found it so easy to switch gears. In response to American pressure, the government slowly has persuaded the Diet to increase its expenditures for rearmament.

This change has increased or created two sorts of problems. First: The continued opposition of the peace forces, led by the left-wing political elements, which have expressed alarm at changes that to them indicated a drift toward the old militarism. In June, 1984, as the U.S. prepared to equip vessels in Japanese waters with Tomahawk missiles, the peace forces staged a rally and claimed that twenty thousand people attended. Antinuclear groups staged sit-downs around the U.S. Marine air station at Iwakuni. The General Council of Trade Unions of Japan and other pacifist groups appealed to world opinion against the Tomahawk. The U.S. House of Representatives heard and passed a resolution postponing the use of the Tomahawk in Japan until 1985. So did the U.S. Senate. But a congressional resolution has no binding effect; what the Department of Defense would do was not certain. It was all made moot when the measure was lost in the conference committee between the two houses, but the Tomahawk missiles were going just where the Defense Department wanted them to go.

Admiral Sylvester Foley, commander of the U.S. Pacific Fleet, was in Japan in June of 1984, and made the point that the American presence was contributing to peace, the indication being that atomic weapons would contribute even more. His remark was pointedly directed to Mayor Kazuo Yokoyama of Yokosuka, who was urging that the Nakasone government adhere to the antinuclear policy of the past, which forbade the bringing of atomic weapons into Japan. The mayor was something of a pain to the Japanese government, but the cabinet managed to ignore him. So the question was moving to a crisis stage and would have to be addressed openly.

There were numerous other indicators of growing schisms in Japan's society. For example, by the spring of 1984 the matter of "Kimigayo," the national anthem, had become a cause célèbre. The ruling Liberal Democratic party joined the Ministry of Education in urging that all schools fly the rising sun flag and sing "Kimigayo." The Japan Teachers Union (Nikkyoso) charged that the LDP was leading the nation back to the emperor worship system of prewar Japan. With the growing schism, the LDP and the Ministry of Education sponsored a new group, Zennikkyoren, the All-Japan Federation of Teachers Unions, which was actually a merger of two smaller teachers unions that opposed Nikkyoso. At the inaugural meeting in Tokyo in March, Minister of Education Tatsuo Tanaka was conspicuously present. Zennikkyoren immediately declared for Prime Minister Nakasone's educational reforms, which the Japan Teachers Union said would bring about state control of education again. As of the fall of 1984 Zenikkyoren's membership was sixty-five thousand, compared to Nikkyoso's membership of five hundred ninety thousand. But in Japan, once a consensus is reached anything can change with startling rapidity. If the government could convince the teachers that central control was necessary...

The switch of Japan to a new nationalism was nowhere better indicated than in the action of the Socialist party to what its leaders called "a pragmatic approach" to politics in an effort to achieve more public acceptance. The switch came in February, 1984. Until then the party had followed a platform set down in 1955, which established a leftist course for taking over government by the working class. In 1984 party chairman Ishibashi announced a four-part program aimed at making the party more popular. That meant the end of open opposition to the Self-Defense Force, which had been a hallmark of Socialist party policy. This change took some gyrations; the Socialists said they had not really changed their views but were waiting until they had a support of the majority of the public for a phased reduction of the SDF.

There was small chance of that change occurring in the 1980s. To the contrary, support of the SDF was growing fast. Even the Socialists had to admit that in 1984, 70 percent of the Japanese people supported the Self-Defense Forces. And the whole Japanese political spectrum was switching to the right, as the autumn elections approached in 1984. The Liberal Democratic party was openly seeking a consensus for support of rapid rearmament. It had already secured the adherence of the New Liberal Club, a small party but one large enough to keep the LDP in power after that party suffered losses in the late 1983 elections. Komeito, the party of Soka Gakkai (the ambitious Nichiren Buddhist organization), had risen to be Japan's number two political opposition faction (after the Socialists), and its sympathies seemed to lean toward the LDP if it could not hold power by itself.

Besides the schisms that were developing over policies of the past that no longer seemed to meet Japan's needs, other difficulties presented themselves, some of them reminiscent of the turbulent 1920s and 1930s, years in which Japanese militarism came to the fore.

Ethical breakdowns affected every layer of Japanese society. Juvenile delinquency had become a serious problem in a Japan that had never believed it would happen. Teenage sex proliferated, stimulated, many felt, by television shows and movies so explicit as to make a prostitute blush.

Low-yield crime was also a growing problem in Japan. In 1983 eight hundred people committed suicide because they were the victims of loan sharks, and eight thousand Japanese ran away from home to escape such predators. What would seem to be the ultimate to a Japanese came in Akita, where two officials of the prefectural police department were arrested for selling forged drivers' licenses. What was Japan coming to when even the police turned to crime?

This sort of worry helped Japanese increase their gloomy feeling that the direction of the nation was wrong. Polls taken in 1984 showed that a majority or a large plurality of the public so believed.

With all this happening despite the general growth of prosperity in the island kingdom, it was an indication that something was very wrong, that the government had on its hands an unhappy, uneasy public that did not quite know what was wrong with its society but seemed to agree at every level that change had to come. The Japanese people were searching for something basic; given that feeling and a desire for change, there was a growing possibility that someone might once again begin to persuade them that the only way to solve their problems was to secure for themselves a new place of their own in the world.

A not unfamiliar notion—and to many a chilling evocation.

5
The Old Militarists

On the surface Japan was much changed by the 1980s, but still much the same as it was in the 1880s in *spirit*. Not so surprising. After all, one would not look at the American hippies, draft-registration resisters, or at the Yuppies and the corporate hustlers and say that the American spirit of 1776 was eroded, old-fashioned or destroyed. Scratch an American deep and you will find an individualist; scratch a Japanese deep and you will find a samurai. There is such a thing as national character, and through war and peace, it persists. So to get a real feeling for what is happening in Japan and what might well happen, one must consider the Japanese spirit and the Japanese past.

The history of Japan is the history of a self-contained society that wanted to be left alone. Until 1853 the Japanese had steadfastly refused any but the most minimal contact with outsiders. In the fourteenth century the Mongol emperor of China, Kublai Khan, had made two attempts to conquer Japan and had failed. Thereafter the kingdom was left alone until the Portuguese came more than a century later. They and the Dutch were tolerated to an extent out of curiosity and some desire for contact with Europe, but confined to an island off Nagasaki. The persistent Jesuits managed to secure a religious foothold in Japan, but it was not a solid one. The Japanese religion was naturalistic (Shinto) and when Buddhism came in from China and Korea, it took a strong hold. Many Japanese added the Buddhist symbols to their pantheon, creating an apparent confusion that served the Japanese very well.

Socially the Japanese system depended on loyalties, and out of this emerged the system of *bushido*, which was a development of the Confucian system of order through obedience. The warriors, who upheld the *daimyo* class of nobles, prided themselves on their unquestioning loyalty to their master, strict fulfillment of accepted responsibilities and maintenance of honor. In return they had the loyalty of the master, and financial support on a level comparable to a highly paid professional of modern times.

The reward in the code of *bushido* is always death and loneliness, this gloomy philosophy that fits the melancholy nature of the Japanese. National gloom was a serious problem in the years of change after the black ships of Commodore Perry had invaded Tokyo Bay in 1853 and 1854. Then a young group of nationalists from among the samurai considered the collapsing Asian world around them and the problem of maintaining Japanese independence, and they concluded that the ways of the Western foreigners would have to be adopted if Japan was to survive. The Japanese, alone among Asians, began to take the steps that would enable them to escape colonial takeover.

Feudal control of Japan had existed since 1603, maintained by the samurai or warrior class. By the middle of the nineteenth century, big banking families (Mitsui, Mitsubishi, Sumitomo, Yasuda) emerged from the trading families that brought goods from abroad. The warrior class fell on hard times, the samurai numbered some two million out of a total population of thirty million, and with no wars the role of the samurai became more stylized than functional—they practiced penmanship, wrote poetry and appeared at court. By the end of the nineteenth century one could say that the merchant class of Mitsuis, Mitsubishis, Sumitomos and the rest owned the samurai.

Yet the samurai spirit persisted among the best of them, a spirit exemplified by Soko Yamaga, a samurai of the seventeenth century whose writings quintessentially represented *bushido*—the way of the warrior:

> Korea was subjugated and its royal castle made to surrender. Japanese military headquarters was established on foreign soil and Japanese military prestige was supreme over the four seas from the earliest times to the present day. Our valor in war inspired fear in foreigners. As for invasion from abroad, foreigners never conquered us or even occupied or forced cession of our land. In fact, in the making of armor for man and horse, in the making and use of sword and spear, and again in military science, strategy and tactics, no other country can equal us. Within the four seas, then, are we not supreme in valor?

When Commodore Perry came to Japan, his arrival and his demands for the opening of the country to trade created an internal crisis in the shogunate of Tokugawa Iemochi. One element wanted to accept, one wanted to resist. Leader of the accessionists was Naosuke, who signed the treaty with the United States and later with France and England. Such treaties aroused fury among the conservatives, and in 1860 Naosuke was assassinated.

During the next few years the country was divided; in 1867 the emperor Komei died and the fourteen-year-old Meiji succeeded him. The progressive samurai—Okubo, Kido, Ito, Saigo—insisted that Japan must follow Western ways to learn. The Mitsuis and Mitsubishis and other merchants agreed, perceiving where the way to greater wealth lay. And so began the Meiji restoration. The samurai were abolished as a class and given money with which to "set up in business." Since they had been trained as nobles and most of them had no heads for business, this was for the most part a futile gesture.

Following Western ways, the Japanese court organized the military along centralized lines. From the West the new leaders of Japan learned the lessons of centralization. A national army and national navy were established, and national conscription for service became the rule. Many of the old samurai sought military service as a way of life but it was different now; in the new army, for example, the lower classes had a chance to rise in station through successful military service.

A major role in the restoration of imperial power was played by two military clans, the Choshu and the Satsuma. Ito, Inouye and Kido were powerful figures of the Choshu clan. Takamori Saigo and Okubo were important samurai of the Satsuma. Both clans were important in the formation of the army, and the Satsuma were particularly powerful in the navy.

The clans participated in the centralization of political power, making sure the military held control. They were about equal in influence in the army until in 1876 the central government decided to put the final touches on central control and outlawed the wearing of swords by any but members of the armed forces.

This was too much for some samurai, especially Takamori Saigo, who returned to his district of Satsuma and began training his men in the old ways of the samurai. When the government tried to get him back to the capital he refused to come. The next year Saigo did set out toward the capital, with fifteen thousand men. They took Kagoshima, marched on. The government sent an army, and eventually the rebels were driven back to Kagoshima and Shiroyama, where on September 24, 1877, the last battle was fought. The end was symbolic of all that had happened in recent years: Saigo was badly wounded by a European-trained conscript of the new army. To a samurai there was only one recourse: Saigo asked one of his retainers to cut off his head, which the man did with a single blow. The Satsuma Rebellion and the influence of the independent samurai were ended. The rebellion also put an end to the influence of the Satsuma clan in the Japanese army, although it retained power in the navy.

• • •

In 1889 a new constitution was promulgated by a committee of the Ministry of the Imperial Household. It brought something new—proclaiming the emperor of Japan "sacred and inviolable," and reminding the world that the empire of Japan had been ruled by a line unbroken "for ages eternal." The emperor, as head of the empire, combined godship and sovereignty. He was the Almighty, above criticism, and without his consent nothing could be changed. The parliament had little power. The Genro, or council of elder statesmen, had much more in their function as group advisors to the emperor. In effect, the parliament's popular government was subject to the rule of the oligarchy that held power in the name of the emperor. To cement the power with the people, the leaders also reinvigorated the religious systems of the past by proclaiming Shinto as the official religion of Japan. Shinto was chosen because of its simplicity: As one student said, Shinto could be summed up as "fear the gods and obey the emperor." The emperor became for the first time divine. Shinto ritual became part of the educational system. Pictures of the emperor were hung in every school, since education was recognized as a means to the end of training the people to build a strong centralized state. In school classrooms and military barracks young Japanese were taught to glorify Japan's past and to revere the emperor. The trappings of the old *bushido* were reemployed for a new purpose: Civilians and military alike were taught that to die for the emperor and country was the glorious fate of the warrior. People were like cherry blossoms, bursting into brilliant bloom and then falling from the limbs. The credo of the upper class—the samurai—was reinvigorated and reintroduced to apply to *all* of Japan:

> The sound of the bell of Gionshoja echoes the impermanence of all things. The hue of the flowers of the teak tree declares that they who flourish must be brought low. Yes, the proud ones are but for a moment, like an evening dream in springtime. The mighty are destroyed at the last, they are but as the dust before the wind.

This Japanese credo was not easily understood by Westerners, who labored under the additional burden in the nineteenth century of a belief in Western superiority and Asian inferiority. The Japanese were quick to recognize the slight of extraterritoriality— the "right" of Westerners to behave in Japan as if they were at home, with their own police, judges and customs. The foreigners put themselves above Japanese law, and the Japanese did not forgive or forget it. Their politeness never failed, but the resentment against the West grew steadily, even as the Japanese learned and adopted as they saw fit the Western way in Asia.

That way, of course, was colonialism.

The Japanese experiment with colonialism began in 1872 after some Japanese sailors were killed when their ship went ashore at Taiwan. The Japanese pugnaciously demanded—and secured— indemnification from China. The next move came in 1874. The Japanese did to the Koreans what the Americans had done to Japan: sent a fleet to force King Kojong to open the "Hermit Kingdom" to foreign trade. The Japanese secured a treaty that gave them all the rights the Europeans got from other Asians, including extraterritoriality. They learned fast. (They still do.)

By 1893 the Japanese had seven army divisions trained in the modern European manner. Many of the instructors were British army officers. Sixteen military schools enrolled twenty-six hundred students. The Japanese navy consisted of twenty-eight large warships and twenty-four torpedo boats. Indeed, by 1894 the Japanese were ready to strip off a piece of China, just as the British, French, Portuguese and Russians had been doing in recent years. They went to war with China over control of Korea. The modern Japanese forces, built so energetically in the European pattern, made swift work of the outmoded Chinese Imperial Navy and Army forces. They defeated the Chinese navy at sea, the army moved into Manchuria and also captured Wei-hai-wei farther south. In the treaty that followed Japan secured Taiwan and the Pescadores Islands, "independence" for Korea—which meant Japan's right to pursue her territorial ambitions there—and the Liaotung Peninsula of Manchuria.

The Europeans were so impressed by this exhibition of Japanese might that they voluntarily gave up extraterritorial rights in Japan. Might brought respect, the Japanese quickly learned, and never forgot.

By 1900 Japan had become a major military and political power in Asia. Her expansionists wanted control of Korea, largely for the natural resources—timber and ores—and the rice-producing area of the south. The Russians were also interested in Korea, particularly its timber. The British, who were worried about Russian expansionism in Asia, saw in the Japanese a natural ally against Russia and signed the first treaty of alliance any Western power had seriously undertaken with an Asian nation. The Japanese and British divided up whole areas: China (British) and Korea (Japanese) so far as respective "interests" were concerned. They also promised that neither would move against the other, and so Japan gained British support to move against the Russians.

Politically in Japan the victories of the military impressed the public and created enormous prestige for the new officer class. In addition to their military exploits, army and navy leaders had learned to exploit the weakness of the constitutional monarchy. If the ministers of war and navy in the cabinet refused to cooperate with the leadership, ultimately the cabinet could not function. And this lesson learned, the military began to flex its muscles.

The first test came with an effort by the military group to increase the land tax, which was the basic support of the defense industries—industries started by the government—but then sold off to the Mitsuis, Mitsubishis, and the others, laying the foundation for the *zaibatsu*, the combination of financial cliques that would divide up the economic life of Japan and maintain control for the next half-century. They were still, though, supported by the land tax, and so the effort by military advocates to increase this tax. The move was opposed by commoners in the Diet who formed the Liberal and Progressive parties, and they did manage to defeat the increase. All this had two long-range effects: It showed the men of the Diet that they had more power than they thought; it also showed the military that they had to move carefully in their attempt to influence political affairs. On the one hand was the group symbolized by Hirobumi Ito, a diplomat who had traveled widely in the Western world. On the other was the group led by Prince Yamagata, a conservative soldier. Both came from samurai families, shared the same general background. The difference was their attitude toward the military—Yamagata firmly believed in military control of government.

Looking around them, seeing constant European aggression against Asians, the military came to the conclusion that Japan eventually would have to go to war with one or more of these colonial powers to secure itself and extend its own colonial interests. So Japan extended its armament, using the money mulcted from the Chinese as "indemnity" for the loss of the Sino-Japanese War. The Japanese, now determined to become self-sufficient in armament, began to build arms factories and shipyards, extended the term of compulsory military service to three years active duty and nine years in the ready reserve. By 1902 the Japanese defense industry could supply all the needs of the Japanese army. The Imperial Army and Navy consisted of more than half a million men. The navy had six battleships, eight armored cruisers, twenty unarmored cruisers, nine light cruisers, nineteen destroyers and eighty-five torpedo boats. Quite an armada.

Japan was now ready to take on the Russians. While "peace" negotiations were occurring in St. Petersburg the Japanese in a sneak attack crippled the Russian fleet at Port Arthur with brilliant use of torpedo boats and destroyers. On the land the Japanese soundly defeated the Russians in Manchuria, and in the spring of 1905 the Japanese at Tsushima Strait all but annihilated the Russian Baltic Fleet that had been sent around the world by the Czar.

The victory of the Japanese in the Russo-Japanese War had some interesting side effects. President Theodore Roosevelt volunteered to mediate Russian and Japanese differences and was responsible for the Treaty of Portsmouth, signed on the American eastern shore. The leaders of the Japanese army and navy were furious with the treaty—Roosevelt had prevented them from getting cash indemnification from the Russians. The vanquished should pay.

The military had also counted on that cash to build an even more powerful military machine. So began a political grudge held by the Japanese military against America, which was being matched by a social grudge. American workers had been seriously frightened during the 1860s by the coming of Chinese labor to help build the transcontinental railroads. The Chinese seemed better workers than the Irish, who built the eastern half of the railway; the Chinese drank tea instead of whiskey and they produced more for less money. At the end of the Civil War this feeling grew and was matched by the feeling of farmers in areas where Chinese, and Japanese, came to farm.

The result was a series of Chinese Exclusion Acts that drastically minimized the Chinese population of the U.S., and the principle and attitude were extended to the Japanese (they both looked alike, after all). The Japanese did not like it, did not forget or forgive.

By the middle of Teddy Roosevelt's second term he felt constrained to send the "Great White Fleet" of American warships around the world, especially to Japan, to remind the Japanese that the U.S. was a world power. The uneasiness between the two countries was irremediable. The Japanese, who have always, like the Chinese, privately considered their own civilization to be superior to any in the world, were outraged at the constant implications of racial inferiority heaped on them by the Westerners, and most particularly by the Americans and Australians. The American navy began to picture the Japanese as the potential enemy in the Pacific, and the Japanese, never slow to follow suit, returned the compliment.

6

The Rise of the Militarists

One of the basic differences between the Meiji constitution of Japan and the constitutions of such nations as Britain was the separation of military and civil powers. The Meiji government of Japan actually existed on two levels, civil and military. The emperor was the head of each of these arms, but separately.

The prime minister, as head of the cabinet, advised the emperor on civil matters. Within the cabinet were the ministers of war and navy, and they were subject to the discipline of the cabinet, except that those two ministers *alone* had direct access to the emperor on matters they considered of supreme importance. So the war and navy ministers could subvert the prime minister.

In turn, the war and navy ministers were absolutely controlled by the senior officers of the military and naval establishments. The rule was that the war minister and the navy minister had to be active officers of the military—a condition first established by Prince Yamagata in 1898 when he was fearful of civilians gaining control of the military.

After Prince Yamagata left the parliament his influence held; he became president of the privy council and a member of the Genro (council of elder statesmen), which the emperor consulted on all state matters. So the influence of Yamagata's Choshu clan on the army continued. As a senior advisor, Prince Yamagata had a powerful voice in the appointment of generals, and through such methods the Choshu maintained control of the army by appointment of loyal clansmen to the positions of minister of war and chief of the general staff. In 1901 Count Katsura, another Choshu clansman, even succeeded to the prime ministry.

In 1912, political pressure from the Seiyukai forced the government to extend the list of possible war ministers to reserve officers, and a lesson was learned by the army and the navy general staffs: To maintain the sort of power the military wanted they would have to control the parliament even though the army and navy were internally controlled by their own general staffs, which were independent of the cabinet and of war and navy ministers. In other words the army and navy each controlled their own organization, and the two were controlled by the *gensui fu*, or Board of Marshals and Fleet Admirals, and the Supreme War Council or *gunji sangun*. The former settled differences between army and navy, the latter reported only to the emperor. The extent of opportunity for military control was such that if a navy or army minister got out of hand with his peers in the service, the general staff simply ordered him into retirement, removing him from political life. The system—called *niju seifu*, double authority—had been engineered by imperial advisors who wanted the military to have control of the government.

The first major test of *niju seifu* control came in 1913 when the army General Staff decided two new divisions of troups ought to be raised for garrison duty in Korea, which had been annexed to the empire in 1910. Prime Minister Saionji had pledged his government to military retrenchment after the Russo-Japanese War and refused to supply the money. The minister of war, General Uyehara, thereupon resigned, and as a telling rebuke to the prime minister handed his resignation directly to the imperial palace. Saionji tried to find another general to take the ministry but none would, and in the end the Saionji cabinet was forced to resign. The Choshu clan's control of the army had been retained.

The same sort of situation developed in the navy. In 1914 scandal within the navy forced Admiral Yamamoto, a Satsuma clansman, out of office as prime minister. Opponents of the Satsuma then tried to push through an anticlan cabinet under civilian Prime Minister Kiyoura. But no admiral would accept the post of minister of the navy so the cabinet fell—even with a majority of the Diet backing the civilian government.

The entire decade after the Russo-Japanese War was a period of rapid industrialization for the Japanese. The *zaibatsu* grew fast, spurred by monopoly grants from the central government. Then in 1911 the driving force behind the government disappeared with the death of the Emperor Meiji, who had exercised ultimate control of affairs for forty-four years. He was succeeded on the throne by his son Yoshihito, who had few of the old man's qualities and no desire to rule. His detachment opened the way for a new era in Japan in which the senior advisors to the emperor exercised increased control, and political corruption emerged for the first time in legislative politics—a cabinet led by an admiral was forced to resign over bribery in connection with naval procurement.

The outbreak of war in Europe, immediately felt in Asia, provided a welcome relief to the Japanese government from its various economic and political difficulties. Indeed, Japan prospered in "the war to end all wars" more than any other nation, with less involvement and cost. Almost immediately after hostilities began Japan and Britain attacked the German colony of Kiaochow (in China's Shantung Province) and soon captured Tsingtao. The Japanese also moved into the German Pacific colonies in the Mariana Islands (Saipan, Tinian), the Caroline Islands (Truk), the Marshalls (Eniwetok) and Palau. They wanted New Guinea as well, but in this one the Australians beat them to the punch.

At the end of the war, however, the military overplayed its hand (as it was to do some twenty-five years later). Along with the Americans and the British it occupied Siberia on a number of pretexts, including a desire to assist the enemies of bolshevism. But the Japanese lingered long after the others had left; did not, in fact, leave until 1922. The cost of this Siberian occupation was enormous, creating considerable economic hardship in Japan. It also worked politically against the military because the occupation had caused such new troubles for Japan. For the first time, the military felt the criticism of both the government and public.

The war years were marked by growing conflict between the Kenseikai or Constitutional party and the Seiyukai, which represented the military clans. The war brought a strengthening of the popular movement and attempts were made to broaden the right to vote and the participation of the common people in government. In 1918 the elite of the Seiyukai tried to capitalize on this move by bringing in as premier Takashi Hara, the first commoner to hold office.

Once the war ended Japan was persuaded to return Shantung Province to China, but at a price that guaranteed Japan a special trading and political position in China, including long leases on the Manchurian railroads that gave Japan enormous power in that region. By this time Japan was recognized as a world power, and the ambition of the military—well whetted—was much greater than most foreigners understood.

Significantly a large number of extremist, ultranational groups emerged: the Genyosha or Black Ocean Society, whose roots went back to 1881 and the samurai tradition; the Kokuryukai or Black Dragon Society; the Roninkai, the Society of Lordless Samurai. The orientation was similar: a greater Japan, a more military Japan. In the early 1920s came many others: the Toyo Kyosonkai (Society for Life in the East), the Toa Renmei (League of East Asia), Tokai Renmei (League for Development of the Orient), Daidosha (Great Union), Sekishinsha (Red Hearts). One of the most important and certainly one of the most active in the cause of militarism and expansionism was the Yusonsha, founded in 1920 by two very modern young Japanese—Shumei Okawa and Ikki Kita. Okawa, director of economic research for the South Manchurian Railway, a Japanese leasehold developing enormous economic power, was using railroad money surreptitiously to support various supra-national movements. Ikki Kita, the cofounder, was a mover in the Black Dragon Society and an intelligence agent of the Japanese war office in China. The Yusonsha proclaimed its intention of uniting all political factions in Japan to fulfill "Japan's great historical mission in Asia."

Japan was beginning to show the world some of its resentments and aspirations. At the Paris Peace Conference talks in 1919 it had proposed international law to govern the principle of racial equality among peoples. The Western powers sidetracked the issue. Such racial slights fed the extremists. The Yusonsha thrived, proclaiming: "Modern capitalism should be displaced by absolute nationalism ... Japan will cause the white race to retreat from Asia." The message was really addressed to the growing middle class in Japan.

There was, of course, dissenting thought, especially in the universities, with the center Tokyo University. Socialism and communism gained footholds but in a particularly Japanese way, each group giving birth to a counter-group. For example, the leftist Shakai Kagaku Rengokai (Intercollegiate Federation for the Study of Social Science) almost immediately gave rise to the Keirin Gakumei (League of the Principles of Government) with an opposite philosophy. The Communist party brought out the Dai Nippon Sekkabosidan (Brigade for Combating the Bolshevizing of Great Japan).

Of all these the most important was the Kokuhonsha (Society of the Foundation of the State), which was designed to combat leftist movements at Tokyo University. It was formed in 1919, and its founders included Kozo Ota, Major Sadao Araki, Kichiro Hiranuma.

The Japanese responded to organization, and those who would control the nation created organizations, most of them to instill patriotic fervor. The Dai Nippon Butokukai (Society of the Military Valor of Great Japan) had been founded in 1897 to promote the Japanese army. Its slogan: "Exaltation of the Japanese war spirit, and rallying the entire nation, united by samurai traditions, around the sacred person of the emperor." By the 1920s, there were scores of such special groups, each grinding out propaganda aimed to persuade the Japanese people that only a military Japan would be a strong, safe and happy Japan, and that Japan was destined to lead Asia out of the pit of European colonialism.

True, there were also a number of progressives and liberals who spoke out in the ten years following the Treaty of Versailles. The political party that failed to maintain a majority in the Diet should resign, voters having to be property owners was relaxed in 1925, civilian control of the army was put forth and control through the power of the budget was achieved. The army was officially reduced in size, and efforts continued to stop naval armament in a search for an acceptable ratio of naval power with the U.S. and Britain.

New politicians of the 1920s were also men of varying interests. Baron Takaaki Kato, for example, had worked for the Mitsubishi industrial complex before entering politics and had married the sister of Baron Iwasaki, the chairman of the company. After serving as ambassador to London and minister of foreign affairs he became prime minister in 1924. His government was known to the public as "the Mitsubishi government," for the obvious reason.

The Mitsubishis and the other members of the *zaibatsu* continued to position themselves against the military. Kato signed a friendly treaty with the USSR, which secured for the *zaibatsu* an oil concession in northern Sakhalin, and favored a conciliatory policy toward China. In domestic affairs, though, a whole succession of governments of the 1920s took a high-handed approach to such institutions as labor organizations and groups wanting social change. Out of this came such measures as the "peace preservation law," which was no more than an attack on those who sought change and was a forerunner of civil oppression by the central government. The net result of all this bickering, plus the corruption and sense of futility they engendered, cost the politicians the goodwill of the public. And, of course, built the appeal of military absolutism. In the 1920s militarism already held a strong influence on all Japan. Military drill was conducted in the public schools under joint control of the war office and the Education Ministry. Such organizations as the Nippon Senedan (Japanese Youth Association) and the Shojo Kwai (Young Women's Association) drew millions of members with calls for "loyalty to the fatherland and samurai valor."

Continuing the pattern of push and counter-push, the *zaibatsu* continued to gain economic strength and was still at odds with the military, lobbying among the legislators. The military, on its side, wanted military adventures to augment and justify its own size and influence, and now the main effort was toward Manchuria and China while the *zaibatsu* wanted trade and good relations with the nations of Europe and America.

These real differences began, as suggested, emerging *publicly* in the middle of the 1920s. The navy was displeased with the results of the Washington Naval Conference, which relegated Japan to an inferior role among the world's fleets (5–5–3 ratio), but the outrage at home was tempered by economic troubles followed by the great earthquake of 1923 and an attempt on the life of Prince Hirohito—both of which disasters preoccupied Japan until 1924. That year the Seiyukai party split and the Kenseikai party secured more votes than either of the two Seiyukai factions, and the next few years saw the rise and fall of a series of coalition governments. In theory Japan was becoming more "democratized" in these years; universal male suffrage, for example, became the law in 1926 for all over twenty-five. But actually the army and the navy were building and consolidating their forces—much more so the army than the navy.

In 1925 Manchuria found itself wracked by war among various warlords, Marshal Chang Tso-lin emerging in control. The South Manchurian Railway demanded protection, and the Japanese kept increasing their forces in Manchuria until they had a very large and well-equipped army in place there—the Kwantung Army. The South Manchurian Railway, a very rich concern, was colluding, in fact, with the army to build its power in Manchuria. Since the Kwantung Army in Manchuria was so far from home, it had to be virtually self-sufficient, which distance also allowed the generals in Manchuria to be extremely independent in their attitude toward the Tokyo government. The generals were waiting for an opportunity to take over Manchuria.

In 1925 the war minister announced that the army favored intervention in Manchuria, and Prime Minister Kato managed to prevent it. After the quarrel the government fell into a series of struggles between the military and industrial factions: Kato resigned, Minister of Home Affairs Wakatsuki succeeded him, but in 1927 that government fell and the military did come into power in the person of General Giichi Tanaka. Two military adventures followed, both involving dispatch of troops to Shantung Province in China "to protect Japanese interests."

In July, 1927, General Tanaka took a trip to Mukden, Manchuria, to meet with Japanese army officers and industrial officials of the *zaibatsu* in Manchuria and Mongolia, where the Japanese had secured concessions and had built up important business interests, the most important of all being the South Manchurian Railway, which controlled iron-and-steel factories, mines and shipping companies. Mukden was the center of Japanese influence and power in the region, and at the meeting the general outlined his government's position toward further incursions into China.

(Later a Shanghai newspaper published the "Tanaka Memorial", supposedly a factual statement by Tanaka at the meeting outlining the whole pattern of Japanese aggression that developed in the Manchurian incident, the China incident and the Pacific War against the West. Whether or not the "Tanaka Memorial" was real, the Japanese then denied it.)

In 1928 Generalissimo Chiang Kai-shek, heir to Sun Yat-sen's Nationalist Republic of China, attempted to bring Chang Tso-lin's holdings, which extended from Peking to all Manchuria, within the Nationalist framework. Chang fled north out of Mukden. The Japanese suspected that given much pressure Chang Tso-lin would cave in, and the thought of returning power over Manchuria to Chinese hands was anathema to the South Manchurian Railway as well as to the Kwantung Army. So as the old marshal's train was crossing a bridge, Japanese soldiers blew it up.

They put the blame on "Chinese elements," but the charge did not stick and Chang Hsueh-liang, the marshal's son, understood what the Japanese were up to and cast his lot with the "Gissimo" Chiang Kai-shek.

The result in Tokyo was chaos. The whole affair backfired against the Japanese army in Manchuria and against General Tanaka. In the months that followed, Tanaka revealed himself to be inept and corrupt, and he was forced out of office in the summer of 1929. The Minseito (Democratic) party was the strongest in the land, and its leader called for democratic development and friendly relations with all powers. With the fall of the military cabinet on account of its failures, it appeared that the civilians were in firm control and that Japan was headed for a whole new era of peace and prosperity.

Yes, so it appeared.

7
The First Conspiracy

The Japanese era that began in 1926 with the coming of the new emperor was called Showa, from the two characters which mean clear and bright, harmony and peace.

The young Emperor Hirohito chose these symbols of his reign because they represented his own peaceful and scientific inclination. In 1921 he had made a trip to Britain and had been impressed with British institutions, especially Britain's constitutional monarchy. There was every indication that in spite of the absolute power given the monarch under Japan's constitution Hirohito would reign in the fashion of George V of England, and that the parliamentary government of Japan would rule. Indeed, in the last two months of 1928 the new emperor was enthroned and made several pronouncements indicating a moderate future for Japan.

But major change was in the air. The Mitsubishis had advocated friendly relations with China, but another section of the *zaibatsu* now had a different notion. The fall of General Tanaka and their political hopes had convinced the generals that partisan politics did not serve their ends. The Mitsuis were persuaded to support General Tanaka's plans for a militarist Japan, and the support of the Mitsui clan brought pressure on others of the *zaibatsu* to do the same.

In July, 1929, the moderate Osachi Hamaguchi became prime minister, but the military did not go into oblivion. In his days of power General Tanaka had been instrumental in the formation of the Ex-Servicemen's Association (Teikoku Zaigo Gunjinkai). Every district of Japan had a branch with a major general in charge. After 1927 the association began a busy program of propaganda directed toward increasing the position of the military. An even more important organization for the future was the Sakurakai (Cherry Blossom Society) organized by Lieutenant General Yoshitsugu Tatekawa, a member of the Japanese general staff. This group and several other organizations of young officers spread through the officer corps, and within two years about half the officers belonged to one league or the other. The purpose was the same: enhancement of the role of the military in Japanese life, and advancement of Japan to control of Manchuria and China.

The year 1930 opened auspiciously enough. The stock market crashes in America and London were still seen as isolated failures of capitalist society, the sort of event that had been occurring for nearly a hundred years. But within a matter of weeks it became apparent that something more pervasive had occurred, and as American factories closed down and banks failed, the purchase of Japanese goods began to fall off. Japan was soon hard hit by the international depression. In its wake was a surge of activity of labor and left-wing political groups and the development of strong feeling against foreign business and the politicians held responsible.

Another reason for a growing feeling against the United States in particular was American racism. For a homogeneous nation whose people nurtured the idea that their own society was the most advanced and superior in the world, it was an enormous shock to learn that white Americans looked down on them as inferior. The Japanese found that their emigrant relatives in America were forbidden to own land and were treated as second-class people. Japan had begun exporting numerous frivolous and cheap manufactured articles to the West to meet the demands of Woolworth's and other high volume, low-priced stores. In America, Japan was seen as a producer of shoddy merchandise; few Americans looked beyond to the strides the Japanese were making in the manufacture of durable goods and their skill in the ancient arts and crafts.

In the 1920s Japan had seemed willing to work toward international racial equality, a concession for a people with such a superiority complex. But faced with growing racism in the West, the Japanese responded with a fury that was all the more dangerous because, like so much Japanese, it was largely hidden below the surface.

The Meiji constitution of Japan had carefully preserved the position of the old upper classes and offered the samurai new employment in the military. It had bettered the peasants and artisans, although not nearly so much as the others. The most important aspect of the upward mobility was the new opportunity for those groups to improve themselves *in military service.* As for the society as a whole, the imperial system utilized one peculiar aspect of Japanese society—adherence of the individual to the group, and a willingness to follow instruction without question.

The years 1929 and 1930 saw the struggle for control of Japan's future direction reaching a climax as the Hamaguchi government tried to establish the supremacy of the civil over the military. The test came in the London Naval Conference of 1930. After the Washington Naval Conference of 1922 the militant nationalists in the armed forces had objected to the limitations placed on the Japanese. The navy split into the "treaty" and "fleet" factions. The treaty faction held it unthinkable Japan should go to war with the United States given the enormous industrial capacity of America. The fleet group said Japan needed a navy at least 70 percent as strong as the American in order to protect itself against "American aggression." The differences were basic and philosophical. The treaty advocates believed in ultimate civilian control of the armed forces; the fleet believed in military control of the nation. The leader of the fleet faction was Admiral Kanji Kato, who had returned from the Washington conference to preach that what Japan really needed was a naval parity (8–8–8) with the U.S. and Britain and that the hypothetical enemy of Japan was the United States. The militarists took up his message. In 1923 Admiral Kato became vice-chief of the Naval General Staff and with his followers gradually undermined the position of the treaty proponents until in 1930 many Japanese had come to follow the "fleet" faction and inside the navy the so-called young officers almost uniformly accepted the fleet view.

On the eve of the London Naval Conference of 1930 Prime Minister Hamaguchi's intention was made clear when he dispatched a civilian, Reijiro Wakatsuki, as head of the Japanese delegation. When the conference deadlocked over American and British demands that Japan's navy remain inferior to theirs, the admirals opposed the treaty. Prime Minister Hamaguchi then took advantage of a loophole in the constitution: If the navy minister happened to be out of the country, then the prime minister had the right to take up the acting navy ministry until the minister's return. Hamaguchi did so, and the cabinet accepted the treaty. It was an unprecedented seizure of control by the civilians; never before had a matter of national defense been decided without consultation with the military.

Admiral Kato, as chief of the Naval General Staff, protested to the emperor, and the controversy became public. The national press and much of the public favored acceptance of the London treaty in the interest of international amity, but the question remained whether the civil or military should control national defense. The emperor being the final authority, the matter went to his privy council, which in turn referred the treaty to the Supreme Military Council of generals and admirals. Not surprisingly, the Supreme Military Council denounced the treaty, signaling that Japan would have to arm outside the treaty limitations. The emperor's privy council seemed about to take the side of the admirals and generals when suddenly it reversed itself and approved the treaty. The reason was public pressure brought on by the government, the newspapers and internal pressure from Viscount Makino, the keeper of the privy seal and Prince Saionji, both antimilitarists. It was likely that the emperor had given some indication of his own feelings in the matter, although of course outside the inner sanctum of the palace such matters were not discussed.

Under the Japanese government the council interpreted the constitution, much as the U.S. Supreme Court is final arbiter of the U.S. Constitution. The difference, of course, was that in Japan the imperial authority was final—but this emperor was unlikely to gainsay his highest advisory council.

The government victory in the London treaty put the Hamaguchi cabinet in the strongest position ever occupied by a civilian government, but the civilian victory was like a red flag before the generals and admirals, who had never imagined the politicians would be able to defeat them on a defense issue. Continuing the pattern of point and counterpoint, they went into action. And the difficult times in Japan were their ally. The American Depression had cut deeply into American imports from Japan, particularly silk, and the silkworm culture to many Japanese farm families meant the difference between poverty and sufficiency. Battered by want and the incessant voices of the right-wing propagandists that rang through the land, the farmers began to believe the militarist claims that politicians, free enterprise and pacifism were responsible for their plight, *and* that the answer was nationalism, militarism and expansion of Japanese power to other countries. Many of the young officers of the military came from farm families, and they saw the plight of their relatives. Military and peasantry fed on one another's fears. The result of the London treaty, and the "betrayal" of the military by the politicians, spurred the young officers and right-wing patriotic groups to action. Several openly called for terrorist activity against the "corrupt politicians." One such group, the Kinkikai (Society of the Imperial Standard), numbered about two hundred officers, all pledged to secrecy. Its tentacles reached up into the younger officers group in the Imperial

General Staff. The announced aim was to secure reforms "under the standard of the emperor." The real plan was for a coup d'etat to be staged in 1931.

The first overt move was an attempt on the life of Prime Minister Hamaguchi, which failed although he was wounded. Soon, though, he was forced to step down, but to be replaced by the man who had led the government group to the London Naval Conference— obviously no improvement to the military.

Point, counterpoint. Force, counterforce. Pendulum politics. A dangerous, unstable body politic.

The generals were split in their own ranks. One group said to wait until the Chinese had exhausted themselves in civil war, then move in. The other consisted of officers who had been involved in the military adventures in Manchuria and Siberia and was led by General Muto and called Saga, after his hometown in Kyushu. A member of Saga became war minister, as did the head of the Kwantung Army in Manchuria. The Saga appealed to the young officers, and soon had the support of most of their organizations. By the end of 1930 the generals were speaking out in disagreement with Japan's foreign policy and demanding preparation for a great war that would create an empire in Asia. It would be Manchuria first, then north China and central China, particularly the seaboard regions along the Yangtze.

By this time the South Manchurian Railway Company and the Kwantung Army considered Manchuria theirs. The problem was to take that last step to achieve a coup d'etat. But in the face of the parallel growing strength of the civilian government, what specific measures could be adopted? The first, obviously, was to get more troops into Manchuria. The military men rued the day Japan had allowed itself to be persuaded to join the League of Nations, apparently overlooking that only thereby had they secured the old German Pacific colonies above the Equator. The outcome of the London Naval Conference told them how badly they would be hamstrung if affairs continued in that spirit. But if they sent new troops to strengthen the garrisons in Korea, said General Minami, the war minister, "the dispatch of troops from

Korea [to Manchuria] would not excite the Great Powers so much as if they were sent from Japan." "Quite, right," said General Ugaki, the new governor of Korea. "And the Manchurian force ought to be given two more divisions." Yes, said the General Staff, and the military must have another eight hundred million yen for its budget.

By July, 1931, the army's plan for a coup in Manchuria were complete. The next month the young officers' groups fused to become the Kokoku Seinen Shoko Domei (Imperial League of Young Officers), with an announced purpose to invade Manchuria and seize several ministries of the government.

On September 18 the Kwantung Army staged the bombing of a bridge on the South Manchurian Railway, then attacked Chinese troops in barracks nearby, claiming that the Chinese had attacked them. By dawn the city of Mukden was firmly in Japanese hands, and so began a general offensive against Chang Hsueh-liang's Nationalist forces in Manchuria, without a declaration of war, without the approval of the Japanese government in Tokyo. The Kwantung Army, with the connivance of the Imperial General Staff, moved swiftly into the provinces.

The consequence of this rebellious action by the military was the fall of the Wakatsuki cabinet and the rise to power again of the Seiyukai (Conservative) party, which had been regarded as closer to the military in the past. In January of 1932 the Kwantung Army fought the decisive battle with Chang's army near Chinchow, and Chang retreated across the Great Wall. Japan now controlled Manchuria. Seiyukai won overwhelmingly in the elections of February.

Japan had also now entered into a terrorist phase, sometimes called "government by assassination." On February 9 a young radical shot down a Minseito politician as he was addressing a political meeting. The police, who captured the gunman, made no attempt to discover who was really responsible—the Chimei-dan, the Blood League. The next month they assassinated one of the chiefs of the Mitsui organization, a clear warning to the *zaibatsu* to fall in line. The terrorists and the young officers blamed the *zaibatsu* and the government for the interference with military control. Those terrorists arrested told the police the Blood League's motto was "every member kill a politician." It was also clearly shown that the league was a creature of the militarists.

It is sometimes said by Western writers that Emperor Hirohito could have stopped the trend toward military control of Japan had he tried. The fact, as revealed in the diaries of several of Hirohito's inner circle, was that the emperor did try to exercise his influence to restrain the military. Consider these words: "The indiscipline and violence of the military and their meddling in domestic and foreign affairs is something which, for the welfare of the nation, must be viewed with apprehension." They are Hirohito's.

After the Manchurian incident the Kwantung Army forged ahead, dismissing the emperor's feelings with the claim that he was badly advised by his senior councillors. The puppet state of Manchukuo was established, and the generals told Pu Yi, heir of the Manchu emperors, that he would be emperor of Manchukuo. When Pu Yi objected, General Itagaki told him that he was at the mercy of the Japanese and if he objected, he, Itagaki, could do as he liked.

The occupation and development of all Manchuria continued apace. The surge came to a head on May 15, 1932, when groups of young officers attacked the cabinet offices, police headquarters and several banks, and they killed Premier Inukai. The young officers then surrendered, demanded a public trial and used it as a podium to expound the military view: The nation could be saved from ruin only by destruction of the Western-oriented political system and the *zaibatsu*. Their declarations aroused much sympathy in Japan, and even the prosecutors treated them as though they were patriots, not criminals.

With its rise to influence and then power, the army naturally began to establish traditions that would strengthen its structure and its hold on Japanese life. Reaching back into the past, General Sadao Araki and the others of the military oligarchy began embellishing the concept of *bushido*. After the seizure of Manchuria

Araki urged all Japanese to cast aside the saber of the Western world and return to the Japanese way of the samurai, to learn the use of the samurai sword and to wear the sword. The mysticism of *bushido* was developing fast. The Yasukuni Shrine became one of the most famous of swordsmithys, where master smiths forged the fine steel with methods that dated back to the thirteenth century. A junior lieutenant might earn only twenty dollars a month but he was willing—eager—to pay five hundred yen, over a hundred dollars, for a fine samurai sword. If necessary he would even go to the moneylenders.

In such fashion were the traditions of *bushido* reborn in the Japanese army in the 1930s.

In 1933 the Japanese army occupied the north China region of Jehol. By March international repercussions were such that the Japanese government decided it must withdraw from the League of Nations to avoid embarrassing sanctions. The emperor objected, but when it became obvious the withdrawal was inevitable, he tried to show his feelings in his two points to be included in his Imperial Rescript of Withdrawal: 1) That it was regrettable that Japan was placed in the position of being forced to withdraw. 2) That even though Japan withdrew, she would continue to cooperate with the league. When these were watered down by the cabinet he tried two more points. One indicated that Japan would continue to work for world peace, the other that "the civil and the military should work in harmony in their respective spheres and should avoid intruding into each other's affairs." This was meant as a warning to the generals, who ignored it. The wording was changed, diluting the world peace motif and stating that "military and civilian officers must adhere to their designated duties."

In spite of the emperor's attempts to bridle them, in Manchuria the army was constantly making incursions into the USSR, their apparent purpose being to create so much trouble that the civil government would be obliged to support the expansion of military power.

The emperor still tried again to stop the tide. After the China incident began at Marco Polo Bridge in North China on July 7, 1937, he urged restraint, and War Minister Sugiyama proposed a statement to the U.S. and Britain that Japan had no territorial ambitions in China.

"You say this," said the emperor, "but can you control your subordinates?"

"Yes," said Sugiyama.

The emperor suggested that the war minister issue a statement to all foreign correspondents in Tokyo to the effect that the empire had no territorial ambitions. Sugiyama was pushed into a position of complying, but it made no real difference. The military juggernaut pressed on.

In 1937 the generals established a new system of control through Imperial Headquarters—Daihonei—which was supreme command. The emperor was to attend their formal meetings, but it had become all but pointless for him to try to take exception to the behavior of the generals. All that resulted was circumlocution and frustration, and danger for anyone who sided with him. There was even danger that if the emperor was considered too troublesome he would be deposed and an imperial prince would be put in his place.

The imperial system established by the Emperor Meiji to maintain imperial control was, it became clear, no stronger than the man who wielded it. Meiji had made it work for him; his son had not even tried to make it work and had allowed the generals to dream of seizing power. Hirohito was wedded to parliamentary democracy in a way that Meiji had never been. He simply was not equipped to take the conspiratorial measures necessary to wield power in the old way.

In 1938 the emperor told War Minister Itagaki that he thought the war with China ought to be ended. The generals told him they would fight on until Chiang Kai-shek was defeated.

In 1939 strong groups in the army demanded a military alliance with Germany and Italy. The emperor objected. So did the civil government. General Oshima, the Japanese ambassador to Berlin, drafted such an agreement and told the Germans that if England and France fought Germany and Italy, Japan would fight England and France. The emperor demurred: "The action of the ambassadors ignores the supreme authority of the emperor," said he. Foreign Minister Arita could only stand and look at the floor. The emperor's authority continued to be ignored.

In July 1940 the moderate government of Admiral Yonai resigned under militarist pressure. The army wanted Prince Konoye to be the new prime minister—his war minister was General Hideki Tojo, one of the Kwantung clique, and his foreign minister was Yosuke Matsuoka, an ultranationalist civilian.

The pieces were in place, the ducks were lining up. The civil government had become a pocket-piece of the army. The *zaibatsu* firms, their eyes on the main chance, had made their accommodation with the militarists, who needed them to produce the implements of war. By the late 1930s Mitsui, Mitsubishi, Yasuda and Sumitomo were in control and had their understanding with the generals. In 1940 the emperor expressed his displeasure when the Japanese officially recognized the puppet government of Wang Ching-wei in Nanking, spoke harshly to War Minister Sugiyama, who tried to crawfish out of the conversation without really answering the emperor's questions. Steadily the war partisans had pushed out the peace partisans in the government and inner circle of the Imperial Palace, leaving the emperor very much isolated. Under the constitution he still had great power, but he had been maneuvered into a position where he could not use it.

After the treaty with Germany and Italy was signed, the emperor warned Prince Konoye that America would stop shipments of oil and pig iron to Japan, and asked him if he were prepared to endure the "darkness and difficulty." Konoye said he was. It hardly mattered. By now there was no stopping the generals. Konoye, pressed by the extremists in the army, allowed the Japanese army to move into Indochina on the night of September 22, 1941. The generals had long since secured the adherence of the navy in the Shanghai incident of 1932, and thereafter, in spite of the urgings of Admiral

Yonai, Admiral Yamamoto and others of the "anti-fleet" faction of the navy, the militarists solidified control.

On September 5, 1941, the Japanese cabinet decided that unless the Americans made serious concessions in the coming negotiations in Washington they would attack the U.S. Preparations were begun. The emperor learned this almost by mistake and was furious. General Sugiyama, who was war minister again, told him that in case of war, the operations in the Pacific should be concluded in three months. The emperor reminded him that Sugiyama had said that the China incident would last about a month. Where did Sugiyama get the confidence to say three months? Sugiyama did what so many Japanese officials had done in these years; he simply hung his head in the imperial presence and did not reply. Then he and the navy minister promised the emperor that first priority would be on diplomacy, when in fact they had no such intention.

"... Why did I not prevent the war before it began?" the emperor asked rhetorically after 1945. "Indeed, this seems superficially a reasonable argument. But in fact it was not possible."

The generals had managed to isolate the emperor just as certainly as had the old samurai isolated a series of emperors, who, theoretically, also wielded supreme power. The real difference between the situation that existed under shogun power from the eleventh century to the nineteenth and that of the first half of the twentieth century was the oligarchic nature of government by the generals. Only when Prime Minister Tojo lost the confidence of the generals and the admirals with the fall of Saipan did his government lose the support it needed to stay in power.

Tojo's fall in 1944 did not mean the immediate fall of the militarists. They had hedged themselves with so many implements of control that their downfall could come only with a new great crisis, which was precipitated by the almost simultaneous dropping of the atomic bomb and the Soviet armies on the Japanese doorstep. Only in such an overwhelming crisis was the emperor able to exercise control.

It hardly boded well for those looking to a permanent reduction in the military and return to independent imperial control. How many such crises could there possibly be in which the military would be so thoroughly humiliated? And posed against such an unlikely eventuality was the deeply ingrained tradition of the "old ways," the military spirit of *bushido*.

True, though in the beginning the Meiji school emphasized the military, supernaturalism, obedience and the spirit of *bushido*, in the early 1900s the emphasis changed somewhat. Textbooks promoted the need to achieve a great Japanese civilization. Japan had already accomplished much, coming out of a feudal period and in thirty-five years achieving the respect of European powers, defeating China in a war and establishing an empire (Korea and Taiwan and adjoining islands). The textbooks of 1903 even show a friendliness toward the Western powers, an ambivalence toward military authority. Emphasis for the schoolchild was on creation of a high culture through good manners, enterprise and intellectual achievement. The sort of military hero lionized was the self-sacrificing soldier. Second-graders read of the young bugler in the Sino-Japanese War who died in battle still holding his bugle to his mouth, calling the troops forward.

But even these restrained texts pointed with great pride to Japanese accomplishments and indicated that Japan's international prestige had been gained by her military feats. By 1910 Japan had won the Russo-Japanese War and many of her leaders were annoyed with the United States for having intervened to deprive her of cash indemnification from Russia. Anti-Oriental sentiment was running high in the United States and Australia. Textbooks were revised to reflect a growing nationalistic sense of power. Japan must look inward for guidance. The emphasis changed to patriotism, loyalty to the emperor and militarism. Pupils were exhorted to incorporate the military spirit of *bushido*, the way of the warrior, into their daily life. Much was made of the Imperial Rescript to the Military of 1882 that described the soldier as the willing slave of emperor and nation, at all times prepared to give his life, to obey orders without question. A poem in the sixth-grade reader shows what *bushido* was supposed to mean to every Japanese family:

The family speaks to the departing soldier son:

First, the father:

Advance, advance, swiftly advance.
Your old father has one hope:
Serve your country heroically
Give to your house the honor of filial piety.

Then the mother:

Before you go, wait a moment, my child.
Your old mother has one wish:
If you go into the army, take care of yourself.
Even if you die by a bullet, don't die from disease....

Then the younger brother:

I am happy, happy because of your bravery.
I am the younger brother of an enlisted soldier.
I will follow you later;
Elder and younger brother,
Let's strike the enemy together.

Then the younger sister:

I, your younger sister, will manage the house,
Assist younger brother and our parents;
Don't worry about things at home.
Come, go forward for the good of the country.

The departing hero replies:

Good-bye, good-bye! Mother and father good-bye...
I will give my life bravely
And attack the enemies of my country.

Gallantly, heroically, the soldier leaves home.
The whole household encourages him.

The spirit of valor goes with him;
Human emotions are left behind
As he separates courage from softness to become a man.

So *bushido*, the way of the warrior, had a part for every member of the family to play.

After the end of World War I Japan saw herself in a more important role in a more complex world society. She had been one of the victors in the war and had profited territorially—much of the old German Pacific empire became Japan's under that League of Nations mandate. Japan was one of the Big Five world powers but the others were not willing to give her proper due. Japan's textbooks reflected a wariness of the world about her.

The salvation of Japan against the Mongol invaders was celebrated in the story of the Divine Wind—kamikaze—that blew away Kublai Khan's ships. A poem celebrated the nation as Great Japan—Dai Nippon—a country that had never been defeated in war. The Yasukuni Shrine, the spiritual resting place of the departed warrior, was signally honored.

If Japan's attitude toward the West was deeply suspicious, her attitude toward China was contemptuous. Japan, said the textbooks, would create a new empire, lead the development of East Asia. Children were exhorted to "respect the national anthem—"Kimigayo"—and be prepared to sacrifice life for country and Emperor." By 1934 the *sakura*—cherry blossom—was celebrated as symbolic of the samurai and *bushido*. The rising sun flag, the samurai sword, warships steaming bravely through the sea and a dozen other military symbols graced the pages of the textbooks. The reading sections were heavily laced with hero stories, and as the heroes committed acts of valor they shouted out "banzai"—cheers—and "tenno heika banzai"—long live the emperor.

The full panoply of military virtues was displayed in the texts; the best soldiers were those who disciplined themselves at all times and were willing to sacrifice themselves at any time. The implication was clear that Japan was surrounded by enemies and potential enemies and must rely on the supreme loyalty of its citizens to survive.

From the moment of induction into the service the recruit was a soldier whose life belonged to the nation and the emperor. And "not only the Imperial Army but the entire nation regard our emperor as a living god," General Senjuro Hayashi told American author Hillis Lory in 1937. "For us it is not a question of historical or scientific accuracy. It is an article of national faith."

Fanaticism had become the Japanese way of life, particularly for the military. For example, it was the custom in the army to read the Imperial Rescript to Soldiers and Sailors on special occasions. In 1937 on the date of discharge of the soldiers of the Sixty-first Infantry regiment of the Fourth Division who had completed their second year of service, Lieutenant Jiro Ushiroku was chosen to read the rescript to the troops. It was the morning of November 30. Ushiroku ascended the special platform on the parade ground, and the men of the regiment formed a hollow square around him. The soldiers bowed and worshiped the emperor. They sang the national anthem, "Kimigayo." The regimental adjutant presented a copy of the rescript to the commanding officer. It was covered with a purple cloth and handled with reverence. The commanding officer handed it to Lieutenant Ushiroku, who read the document from beginning to end, and then the troops retired.

The next morning the body of Lieutenant Ushiroku was found slumped over his desk in the company headquarters. He had committed suicide. The reason: he had made an error in his reading of the rescript. Instead of saying "abide by my instructions" he should have read: "following our instructions." It was the sort of error that the Japanese language made easy to commit. No one else had even noticed it. But Lieutenant Ushiroku was so overcome with guilt that he killed himself. He left a note to his superiors:

> Now then the fact that a commissioned officer who should be the essence of the military spirit had forgotten the Imperial Rescript which no soldier should forget for the space of an instant is not only the acme of shame and disgrace, it also

destroys the moral teachings of the regimental commander and all of my superior officers. My shame and remorse are boundless and unbearable. For four years I was brought up in the *Ichi-ga ya* school for moral training, so although it may be a mistaken idea, I have decided to throw away my life and live again in righteousness...

"I am deeply moved by Lieutenant Ushiroku's magnificent sense of responsibility," said his general. And as far as his fellow officers were concerned, the lieutenant's soul had flown to the Yasukuni Shrine to join those of other soldiers who had died in the line of duty.

The 1930s saw a doubling of this fanatical approach by the Japanese military leaders. It made for superior soldiers. As the Japanese later showed in the field, give a soldier a few pounds of rice, a little tea, medicine against malaria and chlorine tablets to purify his water and he could subsist for a month. He could also march farther and longer than the soldier of any other army and fight under unbelievable handicaps. Despite the uniform, which was ill-fitting and baggy on purpose so as not to give undue attention to clothing, his personal equipment was adapted to the terrain in which he was operating. In the north he wore a dog-hair overcoat and fur-lined mittens. In equatorial climates he wore a green cotton tunic and trousers or less. Foreigners who were inclined to laugh at the bandy-legged little brown men in tennis shoes soon stopped when they saw them in action.

And if he failed? Then the Japanese soldier knew that he must die. For, as General Araki put it, "The soldier of Japan has but two alternatives, a victory of honor, or a death of honor." Never could he retreat or surrender. A surrounded detachment was not permitted to call for help. The most the commander could do was report the facts.

By the end of the 1930s, through the schools, through the press and through every social medium the Japanese people were told that they were a superior race. The old legend of the sun goddess was now offered as actual truth: The sun goddess sent her grandson down to rule Japan. His time and that of his children was spent in consolidating the Japanese tribes. His great, great grandson was Jimmu Tenno, and for the next 2,600 years the family ruled Japan, up until and including the current Emperor Hirohito. The Japanese were the chosen people, superior to all others in the world. Under the standard of the emperor, any action they took to further his and the nation's ends was acceptable. Thus, the sneak attack on the Russian navy at Port Arthur that opened the Russo-Japanese War was seen by the Japanese as laudable. So were the sneak attacks carried out against the Americans, and the British and Dutch, in 1941. A people without peer need not conform to the mores or standards of inferiors.

After Pearl Harbor, the schoolbooks depicted the Americans and British as principal enemies. "Should there remain in Japan the elements who are obsessed by liberalism, which is the enemy's specialty, it will impede the successful conduct of the war seriously. Liberal ideas must be completely eliminated if the war is to be prosecuted successfully."

The office of the Imperial Army's inspector general of education dictated the content of texts, and young military officers were assigned to the editorial division of the Ministry of Education. Tokutome Hideyoshi, relegated to a small place as "statesman" in the past, now blossomed forth as the first Japanese empire builder, whose ambition was to create a Greater East Asia Co-Prosperity Sphere in the sixteenth century. And as the war worsened for Japan, the adulation of the spirit of self-sacrifice was increased.

By 1944 it had become apparent to any thinking officer in a high position that the war was lost. And yet this realization did not bring about a loss of morale.

"There is no way out now except to meditate on the glories of the emperor, who will somehow save Japan," said one admiral.

"Japan has lost the war. We must fight on for salvation, but in the end we must lie quiescent for a hundred years," said another.

In these desperate days, the hero was the soldier or sailor who gave his life to strike a blow against the enemy, no matter if he failed. The kamikaze spirit was idolized. Younger brothers declared their eagerness to follow their elder brothers to a soldiers' life that they might show self-sacrifice.

So from the China incident of 1937 onward, Japan was bent on a course of conquest, led by the militarists, who had gone beyond the point where anyone in Japan could control them. Even when they had lost the war and virtually everyone knew it, the system they had imposed dragged the nation onward to destruction. The militarists had wrought too well for the lessons to be unlearned in a matter of months.

10 | You can see where the uniforms came from. American Air Force and Japanese Air Defense Force generals review the troops.

11 | Eta Jima Self-Defense Force Maritime Force officers' candidate school. This is the Naval Academy built by the old Imperial Navy around 1885.

12

13

14

12 | Japanese Air Defense Force jet over Mount Fuji.

13 | A Japanese jet pilot gives the thumbs up before takeoff.

14 | Air Defense Force jets lined up for maintenance. The techniques are the same as those of the U.S. Air Force.

15 | Every air force has its precision fliers. This is the show unit of the Japanese Air Defense Force.

16 | Japanese Maritime Defense Force seawomen on parade.

17

17 | Air sea rescue is an important part of the Maritime Defense air service.

18 | A floating bridge of the Japanese Ground Defense Force engineers. Regular maneuvers in the inland waters of Japan keep these troops ready.

18

8

The New Militarism:
The Self-Defense Forces

On July 8, 1984, the Japanese SDF celebrated its thirtieth anniversary. The ceremonies were simple and restrained and almost entirely confined to local events at SDF garrisons and bases throughout Japan. The SDF did not want to call attention to itself in the growing debate over the military role being forced on Japan, in part, by the United States.

During the summer the efforts of the defense force were concentrated on achieving a higher level of combat readiness and a sustained fighting capacity. The Japanese were taking seriously the new role of responsibility their government had accepted for them, of being prepared from now on to defend a "limited, small-scale aggression in cooperation with American forces." What the American role in such an action would be was spelled out in a secret operational agreement reached in November of 1984. Theoretically, the potential enemy was the USSR, but why would the USSR—if it launched any action at all—confine it to a "small-scale aggression"? That sounds much more like something either one of the Korean states might attempt. In fact back in 1946, when discussing the American demand for "total demobilization," sev-

97

eral cabinet ministers pointed to future dangers from attack by Korea as a basic reason for keeping a Japanese defense force. As of the fall of 1984 the attempt of the Japanese government to regularize its relations with the Republic of Korea turned out to be less of a success than a warning about the depth of the distrust that exists between Koreans and Japanese. Premier Nakasone did his best to bring about an understanding, as he had done success- fully with China, certainly as much a victim of the old Japanese militarism as was Korea. Nakasone had made a visit to South Korea in 1983, and President Chun Doo Hwan visited Japan in 1984.

What the South Koreans wanted from the Japanese in 1984 was an abject apology for Japanese conquest and occupation of their country as part of the Japanese empire for thirty-five years from 1910 to 1945. They did not get it; the Japan of 1984 had grown extremely sensitive and ever less willing to continue to bear the heavy burden of guilt forced on it by the victorious Allies at the end of the Pacific War.

The best Chun could get from Nakasone was indication that Japan was "searching its soul" over the trouble and "ruinous dam- age" it had caused in Korea during the occupation and an implied promise that the road of the old militarists would not be taken again. Emperor Hirohito, a good weathervane as to Japanese sen- timent, mumbled salubrious comments to President Chun, but stopped considerably short of donning a hair shirt as many South Koreans, especially the media, would have liked. In the ten years past, the emperor had made three statements about the Pacific War, all of which bore the ring of authenticity. In 1975, visiting the United States, the emperor referred to World War II as "that most unfortunate war, which I deeply deplore." Postwar discov- eries of diaries and documents show that Hirohito had indeed deplored the prospect of war with the Western powers before it came, and never changed his view.

The emperor's second pronouncement on the war was to Chinese Communist Prime Minister Deng Xiaoping in 1978, when he spoke of "unfortunate events" in the relations between China and Japan. That second statement was much less strong than the first, but seems to have represented the emperor's honest opinion. He never did have the depth of feeling about the China war that he had against the broader Pacific War.

In September, 1984, the emperor told South Korean President Chun, "It is indeed regrettable that there was an unfortunate past between us for a period in this century, and I believe that it should not be repeated."

Given the realities of Japanese life in the 1980s it would be hard to expect a great deal more. It is not surprising that the Japanese have found it difficult to be expected to rearm, to break down the new attitudes and restraints pushed on them by the Americans in 1945, *and* at the same time to wear the albatross of responsibility for the Pacific War with any conviction.

Privately, many Japanese believed the Koreans came out of the occupation by Japan much better off than they went into it, at least in terms of industrial and agricultural wealth and potential. The Japanese were also extremely conscious of the changing nature of the face of Asia, and the new role being urged on them as a reemerging military force. Prime Minister Nakasone did an effective job of dealing with the Chinese a few months earlier. Out of those discussions came a sense of a real new relationship between Beijing and Tokyo. That relationship was pointed toward closer ties between Japan and North Korea, a matter that worried the South Koreans.

The Japanese saw that their interests in 1984 were already diverging from those of the United States. In discussions with the South Koreans, Nakasone brought up the significant and growing trade relationship between Japan and North Korea. By 1985 Japan still had no diplomatic relationship with North Korea, but the South Koreans expressed concern about the real possibility. The Japanese smiled and said no changes were planned *unless there were changes in the international situation.*

Typically, the North Korean government reacted pugnaciously

to the South Korean-Japanese meetings and to the statements made "to this pro-Japanese stooge from this emperor who was a war criminal and has no real powers."

In that assessment that the role of the emperor of Japan had changed, as the constitution and the publicity indicated, to an almost purely ceremonial role, the world seemed to concur in the 1980s. But how valid was it?

After Hirohito came to the throne his major exercise of power, as noted, had been to end the Pacific War. America imposed on Japan a new constitution that established "legally" the role of the emperor as no more than constitutional monarch. But the Japanese themselves made the changes, and if they so decided, they could reverse those changes. By 1984 many of the changes from the American occupation had been altered, and more were under scrutiny by a nation that was once again feeling a sense of destiny.

Except for nuclear weapons, Japan's SDF in the 1980s was, on a small scale, as modern as any in the world. It was also a mark of the enormous change in the Japanese official attitude toward militarism that for the first time, in the summer of 1984, the Japanese atomic scientists began talking about their ability to produce nuclear weapons in a matter of months, if they were so inclined. They still had not yet reached the point of announcing that inclination, but how far they had come since the days of Hiroshima and Nagasaki! For ten years after 1945 the subject of atomic weapons was taboo; citizens could be arrested for discussing them.

In the five-nation war games carried out in the Pacific in the summer of 1984, Japan fielded a force second only to that of the United States, and considerably larger than those of Canada, Australia and New Zealand. It included modern destroyers, armed with antisubmarine weapons and air defense missiles, helicopter ships and land-based antisubmarine patrol aircraft. The Japanese forces operated as a unit. In other words, the Japanese navy was for the first time afloat again, a perfectly modern navy. The matter of size had to be considered as one that could be adjusted easily;

when one examined the sources of the Japanese armament the old names of Mitsui, Mitsubishi and the other war matériel manufacturers of the *zaibatsu* years kept coming up. There was a difference, of course. For example, Mitsubishi built the F-15J Eagle fighter plane, in 1984 rated as the best in the world, under license from the McDonnell Douglas Company of the United States. But did anyone seriously believe that somewhere in the Mitsubishi beehive there were not plans for Japanese aircraft? Or was the world to believe that the aircraft industry that produced what was the best fighter plane of the early World War II years (the Zero) had lost its creative powers? Mitsubishi was also building warships as of old, and tanks. If for some reason Japan were "to go it alone," as her military leaders decided in the 1930s, all the technology was there, along with research and development about which the outside world knew nothing.

As military writer Masanori Tabata put it in discussing the SDF in the summer of 1984:

"Not only Mitsubishi, but also many other descendants of prewar giant *zaibatsu*-affiliated firms produce and import weapons and other hardware for the SDF. Revival of militarism is hardly conceivable in today's Japan, but a sort of military-industrial complex [compare Eisenhower's departing words] has already grown into a political reality, just like the other industrial powers of the West."

The first clause of that last sentence was a kowtow of sorts to Washington that was common to any Japanese writing on the possibility of a new militarism. It was one thing to discount a revival of militarism in 1984 Japan, but what about 1994 Japan? The 1980s Japan can be compared roughly to that of the early years of the Meiji restoration. In the 1860s Japan began emerging from feudalism. In the 1960s Japan was emerging from stagnation created by military defeat and occupation by foreign forces. In both instances it was assisted by Western powers. In the first case, eventually Japan's perceived interests first parted from those of her benefactors and then ran counter to them. That eventuality in the 1980s was just becoming perceptible in the course of developments in the Pacific, and the attitudes of the United States, which, until President Nixon's breakthrough, had remained unchanged since the 1940s. Nixon made the breakthrough with China. Under his successors the United States failed to show imagination in dealing with Asia. The demands made on Japan in the matter of defense were not accompanied by the other elements that would be necessary if a partnership were to endure. Most important was a trade agreement to assure the continued prosperity of Japan, because without that, the military buildup of the Japanese assumes the aspect of a threat.

Instead of a recognition of the problem, too often American politicians and industrial leaders talk of the necessity of Japan making ever more concessions to American business, cutting tariffs, maintaining quotas on goods-shipments to the United States. Meanwhile loud voices are raised in America against Japanese traders. The Japanese are quite conscious of the statements of Lane Kirkland, president of the AFL-CIO, and other labor leaders who have called consistently for quotas and tariffs to eliminate Japanese competition in the industrial marketplace. A Democratic administration with its traditional obligations to organized labor might be more likely to play the tariff game, but in time of economic difficulty any administration might seek the easy way to stop foreign competition. Franklin D. Roosevelt, the epitome of the liberal, did it in the 1930s. The Japanese have long memories.

Ironically, from a historical perspective, practically everyone in the world, including the Japanese people, was more conscious and more concerned about the nature of the Japanese military buildup than the Americans. In the fall of 1984 the United States Department of State's attitude was expressed by a public information officer of the Far East Division:

"A revival of militarism..." he scoffed in answer to a question. "Japan has a thoroughly modern defense force. It can't happen."

He never went further in saying why the relationship between a technologically advanced defense capability and what the Japanese have always called the national polity meant militarism could not happen again.

When the new five-year defense buildup (1986–90) is completed, the Japanese army—in the 1980s called Ground Defense Force—will have a thousand tanks of the Type-74 Main Battle Tank. (It has a 105-mm gun that was compared by American and Japanese favorably to the Soviet T-62, with its 115-mm gun.) The Maritime Self-Defense Force will have 60 major fighting ships and 16 submarines. The Air Self-Defense Force will have 220 land-based antisubmarine warfare planes and 155 F-15J fighters, plus several hundred other support aircraft. All this being done with about 1 percent of the Japanese gross national product. Even as the plans are being made, the U.S. is putting on pressure for more, more, more.

In 1984 Japan's army ranked only twenty-sixth in the world with its 250,000-man force. But as a retired Japanese general put it in an interview with a reporter from the *Japan Times*, "Both quality and quantity of weapons systems in the arsenal alone do not necessarily portray an accurate picture of a country's defense capability. In terms of morale, standard of training and professionalism, Japan's 250,000-plus armed men are generally rated high."

What the general was saying was indicated by a chart published by a Japanese newspaper, which compared the military establishments of 1945 and 1984:

	1945	1984
Number of soldiers	8,263,000	244,977
Warships	633	489
Aircraft carriers	6	0
Aircraft	9,970	1,320

In 1945 the militarists were bent on continuing the war against the United States, Britain and the Soviet Union with the forces listed above. They were stopped only by the emperor, supported by the reemerging peace faction. With 120 million citizens in 1984 as compared to 72 million in 1945, with an industrial capacity nearly ten times as large, the figures of 1984 on defense can be seen for what they are: an impressive cadre for a military force.

Some might say the most important factor working against militarism was the work of the Americans who did a good job of altering the influence of the military on Japanese society. Renunciation of war and military organization was imposed and accepted by the war generation and to many of the children and grandchildren of the war it became something of an article of faith. In a poll of university students in 1983, 90 percent opposed all military service. Sixty-six percent opposed the Japan–United States security treaty.

The important matter is not what such polls showed in 1984. The antimilitary faction in Japan had official sway for nearly forty years. It would be surprising if the students reacted otherwise to a poll to be made public. But how deep does such opposition go in Japan's society? What about Japan's more ancient and deeply rooted traditions of *bushido*? The warrior's way? Can centuries be wiped out by a few decades? Obviously not.

In the summer of 1984 Chinese Defense Minister Zhang Aiping visited Tokyo, and while he was there Japanese Defense Minister Yuko Kurihara held a press conference:

NATIONAL SECURITY
Treaty with U.S. Essential for Japan: Zhang

Such were the headlines in the Japanese newspapers.

The campaign to reverse Japan's thinking about matters military was well under way.

And the military budget in 1984 began to go up.

Until 1984 the Japanese government had managed to keep military spending below 1 percent of the gross national product. But the way was being prepared in the fall of 1984 for the end of that limitation. In the 1985 budget military expenses were raised 7 percent, which with other funds that would have to be appropriated to give pay raises to Self-Defense Forces personnel, was bound to put the budget over the mark. After that limitation had been accepted by the Japanese the constant growth of the military could be expected with less resistance at each stage. The pressures from the United States were constant and heavy. In an interview with Lewis Simons of the Knight-Ridder newspapers in the summer of 1984 U.S. Ambassador Mike Mansfield said the United States was asking Japan to rearm, not to remilitarize. "There is a difference," said the ambassador. "We would like the Japanese to do more as a sovereign nation in their own self-defense. Period." A nice distinction, perhaps too fine. Near the end of July, Lieutenant General Charles L. Donnelly, Jr., left the command of American forces in Japan to command NATO air forces in Europe. And what were his last words in Tokyo?

"I am concerned that Japan does not yet have enough sustainability."

Sustainability meant the ability of the Japanese to sustain combat. "For a reasonable time," said the general. And what is a reasonable time? No one asked the question and he did not volunteer an answer. But in 1984 the sustainability reached 90 days, which was higher than that of any U.S. force.

Under such a barrage from Washington and Tokyo politicians, the defenses of the antimilitarists would certainly tend to crumble.

They had already begun to crumble noticeably in 1984. The government began a heavy propaganda campaign to persuade the Japanese that rearmament was an essential. "It is the responsibility of politicians to make the people comprehend the [Soviet] threat correctly," Defense Minister Kurihara told U.S. Secretary of Defense Caspar Weinberger. The Japanese Socialist party, which had stood against the Self-Defense Forces and against military buildup for forty years, suddenly in 1984 came about to a backhanded acceptance. For years the Socialists had charged that the U.S.-Japan security treaty alone was a violation of the Japanese constitution. But in 1984 they indicated that the role of the SDF was palatable to them. The reason was simple: The Socialists were trying to strengthen their position with the public of Japan. Only once in the years since the occupation had the Socialists managed to take power as the leading party. Their consistent opposition to the American-Japanese defense alliance made them anathema to the Americans, and to large elements of Japanese society that have long counted on the American defense umbrella to protect Japan in a hostile world. The Socialist turnabout was marked in the summer of 1984 by a Socialist delegation's first visit to the United States to try to bury the hatchet.

The loudest complaints about Japan's accelerated program of rearmament came, as one might expect, from the Soviets. For twenty years the Soviet press had fulminated against "the resurgent Japanese militarism," which they said already dominated Japanese society. In part, Soviet exaggeration, crude propaganda, but there are signs of a steady development of military influence on the government, if not on the people of Japan. Sifting through the customary jargon of Soviet terminology:

"American imperialism," "suppress revolutionary and democratic movements of the workers," "aggressive military policy," "ultra-reactionary," "military clique," and other Communist buzz words in the writings of such Soviet authors as Vice-Admiral A. Gontoyev, one finds legitimate points that indicate the course of the old militarists' development of new influence.

The first coordinated Japanese military program after World War II was "The Basic National Defense Policy" offered by the government and adopted by the Diet in May, 1957.

> The purpose of national defense is to prevent direct and indirect aggression, and, once invaded, to repel it, in order to preserve the independence and peace of Japan for the blessings of democracy.
>
> To achieve this purpose, the government of Japan adopts the following principles:
>
> 1. To support the activities of the United Nations and its promotion of international cooperation, thereby contributing to the cause of world peace.
>
> 2. To promote the national welfare and enhance the spirit of patriotism, thereby laying a sound basis for national security.

3. To develop gradually an effective defensive power within the bounds of national capabilities to the extent necessary for self-defense.

4. To cope with aggression by recourse to the joint security system with the United States of America, pending effective functioning of the United Nations in preventing and removing aggression.

As paraphrasers might say, Japan expressed hope in the UN but not much, and allied herself in the East-West struggle with the United States against the evident potential enemy, the USSR. And one of four points was devoted to the concept of patriotism, which the Americans had effectively worked to eradicate in the occupation years. The pacifism that had been pushed upon Japan had now become a problem that had to be eliminated.

This program called for gradual development of defense capabilities and a joint system with the United States for guarantee of security. That latter, of course, was what worried the Soviets. The revised military doctrine was formulated in the 1970s that foresaw an independent defense posture for Japan. With this were renewed the efforts of the government to counter the pacifism introduced by the Americans in 1945. The date of that revision of defense policy, October, 1976, is marked by the Soviets as the time when "the threat from the north [USSR] was invented by the Americans and the Japanese government to back the further militarization of Japan."

And at some point, it must be said, the Japanese stopped talking only about defense. As one general put it, the line between defense and offense "has to become fuzzy."

In the 1970s the conflicting attitudes were reminiscent of those of the Japanese Imperial Navy in the 1920s and early 1930s: the "treaty" and "fleet" concepts of naval defense. In the 1970s two similar approaches developed in the defense agency: the "Kaihara vision" and the "Sekino vision." Osamu Kaihara, former head of the defense agency who later headed the National Defense Council secretariat, was the author of one view. Hideo Sekino, a retired naval officer, and nationally prominent writer on defense affairs, represented the other.

The Kaihara vision was similar to that of Admiral Isoroku Yamamoto and Admiral Mitsumasa Yonai in the 1920s: that Japan could never win victory in a struggle with any major power. Japan's geography and her natural resource deficiencies make it impossible for her to sustain a war effort. The role of the defense force should be just that: to defend Japan against direct and indirect invasion. There was no way she could police sea lanes (as the Americans wanted her to do). The best Japan could expect against the predictable enemy (the USSR) was that her defenses would slow the enemy long enough for the Americans to come, or for diplomatic demarches to avoid the conquest of Japan. The whole Japanese defense system, then, would concentrate on coastal defenses; no atomic dreams, no missile-bearing destroyer-cruisers, no long-range search aircraft, but escort vessels, minesweepers, coastal patrol ships and short-range aircraft to cope with an invading amphibious force. Japan would accept a total dependence on the United States in matters of defense and allow the Americans to control the bases of Yokosuka and Sasebo.

The Sekino vision, like the old fleet concept of the Imperial Navy, insisted that Japan must be a major Pacific naval power. The Japanese and American interests would coincide as they had for the past quarter-century. *But not necessarily.* And the Sekino vision accepted that possibility, which the Kaihara position rejected.

The Sekino sees the United States and USSR as at a permanent standoff position, maintaining a stable balance of strategic nuclear deterrence against each other, neither being willing to strike first. Thus, the pledges of protection by the United States become meaningless; the United States would never go to war with the USSR to protect Japan. And for that reason, Japan, like the European nations of the North Atlantic Treaty Organization, must arm herself with tactical nuclear weapons. The Sekino vision also presumes that the attack might come from a Soviet client state. In the 1970s Sekino mentioned China. Since then China has done much to remove itself from the Soviet orbit, if, indeed, it was ever really inside except in Mao Tse Tung's perception. Matters have reverted to the age-old status, but the Soviet clients of Vietnam and North Korea remain. Like the Kaihara scenario, the Sekino speaks of Japanese-American cooperation, but there is a sense in the latter that this might not be possible or even necessary. Like the old fleet advocates, Sekino speaks of raw materials from the perimeter of Southeast Asia, Malaysia and Indonesia. The Sekino sees a resurgent military Japan that has learned from its failure in the Pacific War. It maintains a powerful oceangoing naval force. *And* this is the position the American government wants Japan to assume, and the position most naval officers in Japan have been working toward: the resurgence of a powerful Japanese fleet.

The Kaihara, which presents no danger of a militaristic revival in Japan, has already lost the struggle, just as the treaty concept lost the struggle after the London naval conferences of the 1930s. The problem in the 1980s is to prevent the Sekino from becoming a new militaristic nightmare. The stronger the Japanese military becomes, the greater the danger.

As the SDF has grown in size and strength, its reputation has been cautiously raised by careful selective publicity. The Soviets call it the "ideological mobilization" of Japanese society. In 1981 the then-prime minister, Zenko Suzuki, did a little tentative saber-rattling when he spoke of accomplishing the overall program of defense by 1987, which would make Japan, for the second time in a century, third among world military powers. The saber-rattling was when Suzuki also declared "Northern Territories Day," which was a public plaint against the Soviet seizure of southern Sakhalin from Japan in the final days of the Pacific War, and the loss of four islands north of Hokkaido that have always been populated by Japanese.

There is a growing sense in Japan in the 1980s of her own destiny, predictably, as suggested earlier, to be linked in the future more closely to that of China than that of the United States. Since 1974 Japanese and Chinese military men have been getting together for meetings and discussions of mutual problems. In 1984 the Japanese Self-Defense Forces had become a real and potentially independent military establishment, cheered on to growth not just by the United States but by the Beijing government as well. In 1984 that latter development had not been properly appreciated in Washington. It is impossible to believe that so strong and growing a force in Japanese society as the U.S. insists the Japanese Self-Defense Forces become will not begin to flex its political muscles.

9

The Spirit of Japan: Military

In the 1980s Japan has been undergoing a *crise d'identite*. The potential effect of this crisis for the long run is far greater than any aspect of the new defense posture being urged on the Japanese by the United States.

The crisis involves the Japanese view of their own place in the world of the twenty-first century. Having been forced just over a hundred years earlier from a secluded feudalism into the industrial revolution, the Japanese have displayed more than one miracle of coping with the world around them. The Meiji restoration created an industrial and a military power in Japan in just over a quarter of a century. Japan then followed the lead of the Western powers.

Between 1896 and 1942 Japan acquired an enormous empire that included Manchuria, Korea, Taiwan, Hong Kong, a third of China, Indochina, Burma, Singapore, Malaya, the old Dutch East Indies, the Philippines, half of New Guinea, half of the Solomons, and assorted specks of islands, invaluable as air bases in the western Pacific. She even had a foothold in America with her invasion of the Aleutian Islands in 1942, and the most militant officers of the

Japanese army and navy were looking forward to such further adventures as the conquest of Australia, the occupation of the Hawaiian Islands, an attack on Siberia, a drive to the southwest through India and the Middle East to link up with Nazi Germany in the Caucasus, and ultimately an attack on the United States through Alaska.

The Japanese adventure in colonialism brought it flat up against the United States in a war that statistics alone should have told the Japanese leaders they could never win. And there, of course, is the rub about "the spirit of Japan." For the Japanese militarists had convinced themselves, and then the people, that spirit and tradition is everything and physical power and capacity is as nothing compared to it—a concept as old as historic Japan.

Successful generals in all the world's armies have always seen the value of high morale as a major factor in victory, but a point comes in a long war of attrition when morale hardly suffices. Japan reached that point in 1943, when the Japanese, outnumbered and outclassed in military hardware, began throwing human bombs under tanks, human air missiles against ships, and human waves against rockets and heavy weapons. The ultimate was the era of the kamikazes, which began after the loss of the Mariana Islands. The morale of the Japanese militarists never faltered, and in the end the generals were willing to sacrifice the whole Japanese nation to continue their war, and were stopped only by the emperor.

The unconditional surrender in the Pacific War brought an attempt to end the spirit of *bushido* as a social factor in Japan. It was, in fact, outlawed, as were samurai swords and all the trappings of the old patriotism.

Anyone who has recently stood on a street corner in Japan will understand the impact of what happened. On the corner, the Japanese wait patiently for the lights to turn their way. It may be snowing, or the monsoon may be whipping a typhoon through Tokyo. The Japanese citizen waits for the light. One does not see that in Paris, or London or New York. Even in Shanghai jaywalkers dare to amble across the Bund. But not in Tokyo. The Japanese are enormous respecters of authority, and this characteristic is the most important of all in the management of their society. Once determined on a national course, the Japanese follow it wholeheartedly and with enormous energy.

So it was in Japan in the 1940s, when the Shidehara government steered the new pacifist Japan on a course of industrialization. The course was enhanced strongly by the Korean War, which forced the U.S. to depend ever more on Japanese industry and put an end to the attempts to dismember the old *zaibatsu*.

The result was the economic miracle of Japan, which in twenty years saw her surpass most of the industrial nations of the world and take leadership in the fields of automobiles, optics and electronics. In the 1970s the point was reached where her principal benefactor, the United States, became seriously worried about Japan's competition.

In the summer of 1979 U.S. Defense Secretary Harold Brown stopped over in Tokyo in the course of a trip to South Korea and expressed himself as quite satisfied with Japan's level of defense, which was more or less as it had been since the early part of the decade. But by January, 1980, when Brown returned to Tokyo after a trip to China, he announced that the United States was not going to be able to take total responsibility for Japan's defenses any longer because of the upsurge of danger in the Middle East. Except for the nuclear umbrella, he said, Japan had to get ready to defend herself.

This same note was sounded again in March, 1980, when Foreign Minister Okita visited Washington. And it came up again on May 1 when Japanese Prime Minister Ohira met in Washington with President Jimmy Carter.

On June 30, 1980, the Japanese and Americans held a three-day defense conference, in which the American demands were even greater. At the same time a bill was introduced in the U.S. Senate to force *all* Allied nations to increase their defense efforts as the price of continuing American support.

The Japanese respond quickly to stimuli. In the summer of 1980 a survey conducted by *Nikkei*, a business magazine, showed how great had been the change in Japanese thinking about Japan's international position in just over a year. Before 1979, the largest elements of Japanese society considered their country to have become a merchant nation, doing business with all, under the letter and spirit of the peace constitution. The uncomfortable relationship with the USSR was a matter for concern but not consternation.

In the survey, *Nikkei* offered four choices for the Japanese vision of the future:

1. Chomin (Merchant) nation. Defense expenditures would remain at the old levels.

2. Akinai (Trading) nation. Defense expenditure should remain under 1 percent of the gross national product, but foreign aid should be sharply increased.

3. Chugurai (Middle-ranking) nation. Defense expenditures would be increased to 1.9 percent of the GNP and foreign aid moderately increased.

4. Bushi (Warrior) nation. Defense spending should be increased to more than 2 percent of the GNP and Japan should arm herself with nuclear weapons.

When the results were tabulated, 87 percent of businessmen and 83 percent of bureaucrats chose the middle roads, trading and middle-ranking nation. But a change was notable. Two years earlier a demand for an increase to 1 percent of the gross national product for defense had been unacceptable. What occurred in Japan in a matter of months in 1980 was a major about-face occasioned by American demands. It could occur because within the Japanese government establishment were many political leaders who actually believed in the need for a resurgent military power on a full scale. They had been quiet as mice in the later 1940s, no more than tentatively suggestive in the 1950s and 1960s. On November 25, 1970, the celebrated author Yukio Mishima went to the headquarters of the eastern section of the Japanese Self-Defense Forces in Tokyo. Accompanying him to the building were about two thousand of his followers, Mishima having emerged in recent years as an ardent advocate of the old "Imperial Way," the Japan of his childhood, in which the spiritual was also martial. He had spent much of his money to build an organization dedicated to this precept, and now he came to demand of the SDF that it imitate the army of 1936 and seize power, if only for a moment, to show the way, as the young officers had done in 1936. Mishima met an unbelieving audience. He climbed onto a balcony and began to address the crowd. Members of the SDF jeered him. The commander of the eastern section indicated that Mishima must be mad. Mishima spoke for ten minutes. Only the SDF, he said, possessed the soul of the real Japan... "If there is any samurai Japanese spirit among us, we can't wait any longer, we must have a military coup at once."

Greeted by hoots and catcalls, Mishima grew more agitated each moment. Obviously he had prepared himself for this eventuality. When he failed to arouse his audience he played his final card: He disemboweled himself on the balcony in the *bushido* tradition of *seppuku*.

Yukio Mishima achieved the shock effect he wanted, but the results would not have been pleasing to his soul. The majority of Japanese had, apparently, been sanitized. Those who agreed with Mishima could read the signs around them; they knew it was too early to begin to act... they *also* knew that there might come a time when the reaction would be different. For as the spokesmen of the left were saying in the 1970s, Japan's democratic tradition was only skin deep. In the closet where the postwar businessman parked his attaché case at night, might also be found a samurai sword, pushed back among the family relics, but not discarded.

In the 1970s the believers in military power for Japan began to come out of the cocoon, and by 1980 some of them at least were beginning to suggest that Japan needed more power. The approach at the time was careful, so as not to annoy anyone except the Soviets. By example, as of the fall of 1980 the well-known Japanese military historian Hisao Iwashima would say, as he did at a symposium on contemporary Japan at Sheffield University in England, that "if the choice of the kind of future is frankly asked of the Japanese, they will choose a steady course which aims at strengthening a Pacific Basin Community concept, rather than any routes that lead to Japan becoming a great military power in the Asian-Pacific area."

Nothing of concern there, but if history teaches anything, it is that the general attitude of business and the public is responsive to economic and political events. In 1980 a whole series of political and economic events came about as the result of the change in Japanese-American economic relations and the American demand for change in defense relations.

This stiffening of the American attitude, while not definitive in 1980, was still enough to give the Japanese pause about the future of their own economy and their defenses. The American insistence that Japan undertake more of the defense of Asia against a hypothetical Soviet threat showed that the Americans would never again be willing to shelter the Japanese totally under the American umbrella.

So in Japan a national debate about defense posture began in 1980 and continued to gain public attention. Until 1980 most arguments about Japanese defense policy concerned Article IX of the constitution, the section that outlawed war "forever" as an instrument of national policy. After 1980 the discussions no longer centered about the constitution but about a practical military policy for Japan. By 1985 no one but the communists and professional pacifists brought up the matter of the peace constitution's renunciation of self-defense. Even the Socialist party had made its accommodation.

In August, 1980, the Japanese cabinet approved a defense white paper and a diplomacy blue paper, both emphasizing Japan's responsibility as a member of the American bloc and asserting the necessity of a self-defense effort of suitable power to let the Japanese respond to a Soviet threat.

That same summer the Foreign Ministry released a year-long study that asserted: "It is necessary for Japan to contribute toward the strengthening of the free world." This study also signaled the government's willingness to dispatch elements of the Self-Defense Forces abroad.

Beginning in 1980 the Self-Defense Forces showed a changeover to an offensive attitude, which had never been so indicated before. On August 15 a war game called Dawn Exercise was staged in northern Hokkaido, with ground, air and sea forces participating. At the same time the defense agency said that the aircraft would be actually armed from that point on with live air-to-air missiles. The maritime force announced that in future escort ships and planes on antisubmarine patrol would be armed with live torpedoes. One comparison indicated the depth of change: On December 6, 1941, American submarines in the Pacific were still fitted with dummy torpedo warheads and most military aircraft were unarmed. As of the summer of 1980 the Japanese Defense Agency moved over from what historian Iwashima called "extreme caution" to "bolder self-assertion."

What happened in Japan in 1980 is revealing: The militarists began to come out from under the rug of pacifism that had lain so long across Japan. Coming out, they soon found converts in unexpected places:

For many years Professor Ikutaro Shimizu was associated with the pacifist movement in Japan. It was a real surprise for Japanese intellectuals, then, to see the professor advocate, in a series of newspaper articles in 1980, a totally independent Japan that would have her own defenses, including nuclear weapons. The United States, said professor Shimizu, had proved unreliable, and thus Japan must regard her security with new eyes. Since the United States could not be trusted, Japan must develop her own self-defense and offensive capability to reply to enemy attack. He spoke of the creation of at least two aircraft carrier fleets; 17 carriers, 34 antiaircraft destroyers and 85 multipurpose destroyers. The air forces should be strengthened to at least 350 F-15 Eagle fighters. The ground forces should be brought up from 48 armored vehicles to 300. The military budget should be increased to at least 3 percent of the gross national product.

Obviously a longtime pacifist was not going to have access to the studies and concepts that would permit him to make such specific suggestions in the military line. The professor admitted that he had the benefit of the advice of a military science study group that included "the highest authorities on military matters." The professor did not name his authorities, but it did not take much of a guess to determine where they came from. In the 1980s a number of officers from the old Japanese Imperial Army and Imperial Navy survived. Some of the most prominent, such as Mitsuo Fuchida and Minoru Genda (both prominent in the Pearl Harbor attack), could not at first be employed by the Defense Agency because of public opinion in America and Japan, although Genda in particular was sought out by many Americans for discussions on military matters and sometimes wrote for the Proceedings of the United States Naval Institute, the institute being a semiofficial organization. Eventually he did become head of the Defense Agency as government policy changed.

Policy actually had begun to change the moment it was made. By August, 1950, with the Korean War raging, Japanese militarism seemed less important than it had five years earlier, and nearly twelve thousand army and navy officers were depurged, up to the rank of colonel and navy captain. These senior officers had spent their whole careers in the spirit of *bushido*. It is unreasonable and unrealistic to believe that they all renounced the past.

The record of the development of the Self-Defense Forces gainsays any such fairy tale. During the barren years for the Japanese militarists, the 1920s, army and navy officers of Japan comported themselves with great dignity and spartan simplicity. A full general earned $126 a month, a sublieutenant $16. Unless an officer was stationed abroad he had virtually no perquisites, no housing allowances, no per diems, and it was not common for officers to live on post. The physical demands on the officers were the same as on the men; endurance was the name of training. The officers' mess was little different from that of the enlisted men, the food was almost the same. Regimental officers' quarters on post consisted of rooms with plank floors and uncurtained windows. Frugality and simplicity were the rule (see Appendix 1). For this, unintentionally, the Japanese military gained the respect of the Japanese public. Hideki Tojo, for example, although prime minister during much of the war, holding the highest political and military office of Japan for four years, lived frugally and died poor. The corruption of the Japanese militarists was spiritual, not material.

Comparison of the lean years of the Japanese military between two world wars and the post-Pacific War Defense Agency is useful. After 1945 the professional soldier and naval officer came on very hard times. Yet they stuck together. Eta Jima was the old Japanese Imperial naval academy. Its graduates of the years 1933 to 1943 suffered casualties of more than 50 percent during the war. The way in which the war ended precluded any consideration for the fallen heroes or their families, but the surviving graduates undertook to support the dependent families of their dead comrades and continued that practice through the years. Until 1983 all the commanders of the Maritime Safety Agency (new navy) were graduates of the old Eta Jima school, with all its traditions of *bushido*. Although the percentage of former Imperial Navy officers in the new navy decreased from year to year, until 1970 about a sixth of the officer corps was still of the old school, all of the admirals and most of the captains and commanders were Eta Jima graduates, and the tradition was so strong that they still traced their seniority by their Eta Jima numbers.

Between the 1950s and the 1970s, the military profession was not highly respected in Japan. The fringe benefits of the Self-Defense Forces compared unfavorably with the opportunities in business life. Salaries were not competitive. Civilians seemed contemptuous of the soldiers and sailors; because so many students protested, the big universities like Tokyo University stopped admitting SDF members for postgraduate work. Nonetheless the military survived, and many young men sought military service. An air-officer program, through which a young man could enlist out of high school, and after five years of training become an officer, had an application rate as high as forty-four-to-one acceptance. But because of the size of the force, the whole program was small, turning out about fifty pilots a year. This was, of course, a glamour program.

In 1945 when the Japanese army was disbanded along with the

navy, and officers were purged—although many eventually found their way into the police or back into the service—enlisted men of the services were never purged as such. So as the forces began to grow in the 1950s, old members of the Imperial Japanese Army and Navy returned to service.

In the earlier years, as in the United States, there was deemphasis of military matters and emphasis on personal advancement. "Join the SDF and advance your education," was one recruiting slogan. "Join the defense forces and save ¥1.4 million [$3,900] in four years," was another.

In the Self-Defense Forces of the 1980s the *bushido* concept does not exist—not officially, that is. But not even the victorious Americans, addressing a prostrate enemy, could by decree erase a whole national history.

In 1973, James Auer, in a study of the postwar Japanese navy, commented on a growing defense consciousness and feeling of responsibility among young people in Japan. But, he added, "should a real danger be perceived, the situation might change radically ... the racially homogeneous family of Japan might react much more defense-mindedly than foreign observers might expect, given Japan's present apathy."

That was as recent as 1973. By 1980 what Mr. Auer had suggested as a possibility had come to pass. The "real danger" was perceived: The Soviet Union. The invasion of Afghanistan, the bullying of Poland, the destruction of a civilian South Korean airliner in 1983; all had to be regarded as major Soviet blunders if only because of the reaction in Japan. Even the Japanese Communist party was critical of the Soviets. And the last was worst: The blustering Soviet threats against any who approached Soviet borders had to be taken as a special warning to the Japanese, another reason for them to perceive the Soviets as the potential enemy. Then, to add emphasis, the fall of 1984 was marked by several Soviet bomber incursions into Japanese airspace.

Given the difficulties of creating and maintaining a defense force in a nation officially wedded to the principles of pacifism and the outlawry of war, the development of loyalty to the military had to come from within.

The Japanese Defense Agency was organized as a volunteer force, and at the beginning it was called a "civilian" agency. (Legally it still was "civilian" in 1984.) General MacArthur had set out to create in Japan "the Switzerland of Asia." The graduates of the four-year Defense Academy could walk away on the day of commencement and take a civilian job and there was nothing the SDF could do about it. In fact, though, 95 percent of the graduates went on to service. A number of them interviewed by James Auer indicated that they had entered the academy to secure a free university education, intending to quit on graduation. But something happened to them along the way. They stayed in, and after several years of service they continued to stay in. As of 1985, 95 percent of the officers remained in the service, as compared to 38 percent as an average over the past twenty years for those United States Naval Academy graduates who remained in service after meeting the five-year service requirement. The same general statistics applied to the U.S. army and U.S. air force.

A stunning difference. Despite the relatively low esteem in which the Japanese military was held for thirty-five years the military men managed to maintain a high morale. Before and during World War II the Japanese naval academy at Eta Jima maintained the highest educational standards—not just training for naval officers. Admiral Shigeyoshi Inoue, the commandant of Eta Jima, believed in education; the school should impart knowledge, not just skills. Significantly, while even Tokyo University stopped teaching English during the war, the Eta Jima academy never stopped. The real emphasis, though, at the academy was on *spiritual training*— once again, *bushido*. One can say the same of the Self-Defense Forces in the 1980s. Beginning in 1954 with the establishment of the Safety Academy, President Tomoo Maki insisted on "wide vision, scientific thinking and rich humanity." It was a continuation of the Eta Jima philosophy. And the control continued to be that of the imperial era; in the navy, for example, until 1983 when the graduates of the seventy-fifth Eta Jima class were scheduled to retire, the chief of the maritime staff was always an old IJN Eta Jima man. In 1984 the first Defense Academy graduate took over as commander. By then, the principles of the old Imperial Navy had been instilled throughout the force.

So Eta Jima, that bastion of *bushido*, continued to exist, although the difference in 1984 was that most professional officers of the Self-Defense Forces came through the general academy, and then were parceled out according to their desires and the needs of their services to the army, navy or air force. About half the needs—especially army—were met by promoting from within. The petty officer or sergeant in the Japanese military forces always occupied a position of higher authority than did, for example, a petty officer or sergeant in the U.S. forces. The petty officer was regarded as the trained man; the officer was regarded as the thinking man. Consequently until 1945 the top graduates of the Japanese military academies formed a sort of elite through which the traditions of the service were carried on. So it is in the 1980s, although it is not announced or even admitted. But neither was the fact admitted in the old days. Tradition was the secret that had so much to do with the maintenance of a high level of morale and performance among the Japanese military.

The new army's special training schools did away with many of the trappings of the 1930s *bushido*: regimental colors, ballads of the service and other ceremonial aspects that might smack of the old militarism. But at Eta Jima, the naval academy, no bones were made about the efforts to instill the spirit of the old Imperial Japanese Navy into the students. Among things to be revered in the museum were a hank of the hair of Admiral Heihachiro Togo, the victor of Tsushima; a *kaiten* (human torpedo) and various mementos and writings of kamikaze pilots and other suicide specialists. The students sang the same songs that the Imperial Japanese Navy students sang in the old days. Their spiritual principles were those drafted by Admiral Hajima Matsushita in 1931:

    1. Have I lived up to the spirit of wholehearted devotion to duty?

2. Have I been amiss in words and conduct?
3. Have I been lacking in vigor?
4. Have I been fulfilling my duty as I should?
5. Have I been lazy? (See Appendix C.)

The answers, as far as the world was concerned, were remarkably positive. After graduation, the navy men went on overseas cruises. Their deportment was reported as so close to perfect that the officials of other navies found it hard to believe.

Technically speaking, the officers and men of the Japanese Self-Defense Forces had some hard sledding, which was largely dissipated by intensified American training programs of postgraduate officers and advanced petty officers and sergeants. As for the navy, foreign military observers were by 1985 almost all favorably impressed by the standards of seamanship, cleanliness, efficiency and discipline aboard Japanese warships. Officers and petty officers of the old Imperial Japanese Navy complained that there was little spirit as compared to the old days. But just as the navy of Admiral Yamamoto in 1941 was not the navy of his mentor Admiral Togo in 1903, so the new navy of 1984 was not that of 1941. What was important was the degree of retention of the standards of the past.

The old harsh discipline of the imperial forces might be gone, but that was a trapping, not an essential. The essentials were the same—patriotism and duty. (See Appendix C.) And here the warrior's way remained as it was. The potential and basis for a revival of the Japanese martial spirit was in place, the development in only four years of a new image of the Self-Defense Forces was sufficient indication of that. What would happen next depended on how Japan perceived itself in relationship to the rest of the world.

10

The Spirit of Japan: Political

In 1984 out of the closets of the past the Japanese were resurrecting half-forgotten and forbidden monuments to the glory that was in the days of the old Imperial Yamato, empire of the rising sun.

It was going on half a century since the Pacific War had ended and the coals of ignominy had been heaped on a nation that had lost the war and was charged with all the crimes that the victors could put on them. The Japanese who were old enough to remember the war were by 1984 weary of bearing a burden that many believed should never have been placed on them. They had acquired a new respect in the world through their economic resurgence to reach the top of the heap of industrial nations. The demands of the United States that Japan rearm to protect what the American leaders saw as common interests had given the Japanese the opportunity to shuck off the last strictures of defeat. The Japanese, a proud people, were determined to stand up straight at last, even to take exception to the common Allied historical view of the war. Behind the general public, press and politicians were the lovers of the past tradition who would have liked nothing better than to restore the grandeur of the old imperial government. One did not have to conjure up goblins to see how the restoration of the past was bringing back the trappings of the old Japan that honored and obeyed the military. Some might say the effect was no more serious than that of a band of American southerners gathering round a monument to Robert E. Lee to celebrate Virginia Secession Day. But in 1985 the sun of the Japanese pacifist seemed to have set, and the sun of the militarist to have begun its rise.

The signs:

1. One Sunday in May, 1984, Yuko Kurihara, director general of the Japanese Defense Agency, journeyed to Kagoshima to attend a memorial service in honor of Admiral Heihachiro Togo, the victor of Tsushima Strait, who had crushed the Imperial Czarist navy there and earlier at Port Arthur to lay the foundation for Japan's victory in the Russo-Japanese War.

The ceremony marked the fiftieth anniversary of the death of Admiral Togo. For the purposes desired, Togo was the ideal figure: He was two generations removed from the militarists who engineered the Pacific War, and yet he was a bona fide military hero whose virtues represented the sort of Japanese patriotism the leaders of Japan in 1984 wanted to espouse. His great-grandson was a newly commissioned ensign in the Maritime Defense Force. The tradition was being carried on.

The United States, Britain and others of the Western Allies pointedly sent naval officers and diplomats to Kagoshima for the ceremony.

The Soviet Union, equally pointedly, stayed away, and her diplomats complained that the ceremony "reflected the revanchist sentiments in Japan and hostility against the Soviet Union."

They were right on both counts, if not precisely in the way they indicated. Revanchist to the Soviets means the old militarism that seized Japan in the 1930s and substituted military for political control, even to the point of outlawing political parties. That sort of revanchism was not visible in Japan in 1984. What was becoming visible was a yearning for the self-esteem and national pride that marked the Japanese of the imperial years. As for anti-Soviet feeling, it had never been higher in Japan than in 1984, fanned especially by the shooting down in 1983 of that Korean airliner somewhere around Sakhalin, which was Japanese territory until seized by the Soviets as booty from World War II. The Japanese continued to believe that southern Sakhalin was theirs, along with four smaller islands the Soviets also seized. Feeling ran high enough in 1984 that the Japan-Soviet Friendship Hall in Hakodate, Hokkaido, was closed down, as were four similar friendship halls elsewhere. In the view of the Self-Defense Forces, the USSR was the hypothetical enemy and had been since 1960, as all Japan knew.

"I would be happy if the defense capabilities can be improved with the understanding and cooperation of the people of Japan," said Director General Kurihara in his speech at the Togo memorial meeting. The Japanese are a consensus people; they respond best to change when it is introduced to them gradually through a gentle campaign of salesmanship. Director Kurihara's gesture opened a new campaign to persuade the Japanese people that a powerful military posture must be assumed by the nation.

2. For years the Japanese government had been aware of the presence of nuclear weapons on American ships calling at Japanese bases, but the fiction that this did not happen was carefully preserved. In the summer of 1984 the fiction was nearly cast aside. The American atomic submarine *Tunny* came to Japan and in the face of pacifist complaint the Japanese government refused to ask the Americans if the vessel was bearing Tomahawk missiles, which carry atomic warheads. The Americans had already announced that the *Tunny*-class submarines would be carrying atomic warheads. The pacifist movement, once strong enough in Japan to shake cabinets, was unable to stir the public on the issue.

3. The Yasukuni Shrine is as much a relic of the old militarism as anything in Japan. It was the home of the heroes of Japanese wars, and under the state Shinto religion of the war years, it was believed that the souls of all departed soldiers killed in battle went to the Yasukuni Shrine. Millions of Japanese still so believed in 1984.

At the end of the Pacific War, the shrine fell into the gray area of the past, supported largely by the relatives of fallen soldiers. But in the 1980s politicians, particularly those of Prime Minister Nakasone's Liberal Democratic party, began making ostentatious visits to the shrine with the approval of many voters. Some political party men objected but the visits continued. It was a private matter, said old navy officer Nakasone as he visited the shrine in the spring of 1984. Then came a move by the LDP to secure state support for the shrine. The prime minister should make state visits to the shrine, in his official capacity, and inscribe his name and title in the visitor's book, said the LDP.

Spokesmen for other parties said such would be a violation of the constitution, which, like the American Constitution on which it was generally modeled, draws the line between church and state. But that was a smoke screen over the real issue. "Such proposals would pave the way for the state management of the shrine and thereby for the return of the prewar militarism and a revival of Shinto nationalism," said a spokesman for the Japan Socialist party.

4. The Yasukuni Shrine was also the subject of another controversy with another set of unpleasant associations with the past. One of the marks of the old Japanese militarism was jingoism linked with a basic distrust of foreigners, attitudes that had been almost indiscernible in postwar Japan. For a people as homogeneous as the Japanese, they had, since 1945, shown a near-charity toward foreigners, in marked contradistinction to the 1930s and 1940s. One of the key Japanese policies in the Greater East Asia Co-Prosperity Sphere was the put-down of foreigners, particularly Caucasians, and many of the cruelties that led to the war crimes trials, such as the Bataan Death March, were staged to show Asians that the white man was not superior, could be humiliated. In the postwar years all that was submerged—but far from dead.

In the winter of 1983, when Eugene MacDonald and his wife were touring Japan and they visited the Yasukuni Shrine, they were turned back from the shrine's main hall. They had gone inside the hall of worship, the outer part of the shrine. They had followed a group of Japanese through the entrance to the main hall, only to be stopped and told that foreigners were not permitted in that part of the shrine because it was sacred to the Japanese, enshrining the souls of 2.4 million persons who had died for their country. When MacDonald wrote a letter of protest to the press, the officials of the shrine claimed it was all a mistake, and the foreigners were not allowed only because they had not registered first. Neither the MacDonalds nor many readers were likely to believe that tale.

5. In June, 1984, a Yokohama District Court judge found Kathleen Morikawa, an American resident in Japan, guilty of refusing to have her fingerprints taken in connection with her registration as an alien. She was fined ¥10,000 (then about $50). Ms. Morikawa was not just a resident of Japan, she was also married to a Japanese citizen. She objected to being fingerprinted "like a common criminal." The law under which she was tried had been on the books since 1955 but never really invoked until it was strengthened in 1982. The judge held that there was a basic difference between foreigners and Japanese, and that the foreigners had to expect restrictions and some curtailment of rights. That statement represented a new view of the Japanese bureaucracy similar in a way to that of the 1930s. But the fact is that the Japanese have been extremely xenophobic. What was happening in 1984 was a reflection of the Japanese central bureaucracy's new sense of power. Too much strengthening of the central government could create the sort of Japan that existed in the 1930s, when citizens had to bow to the corner policeman. The question hung in the balance in 1984 — an indicator of the feeling toward outsiders, and perhaps more.

6. A tendency toward xenophobia was also indicated in 1984 by a new movement — the National Conference for the Promotion of the Enactment of an Anti-Espionage Act. The movement was launched in 1979, grew enough in the next five years to hold a national convention in Tokyo attended by twenty-five hundred politicians, scholars and intellectuals. Former Prime Minister Nobosuke Kishi was there as were eighty-six other members of the

Liberal Democratic party. They included Masayuki Fujio, chairman of the LDP Policy Affairs Research Council and Asao Mihara, a former SDF director.

Despite Japan's constitutional renunciation of war, putting her in an awkward position to talk about espionage since she was not supposed to have any military secrets, in 1984 the National Conference for the Promotion of an Anti-Espionage Act had already gained a great deal of momentum. At the local-government level more than half of the prefectural assemblies and about half of the municipal governments of Japan had already come out in favor of the movement. The LDP suggested a law invoking the death penalty for any person who collected defense secrets for a foreign power. The LDP tried to push such a law through the Diet, but in 1984 it had still been stopped by opposition party members who held that the espionage act was basically an attempt to control the freedom of the media. Certainly, just such measures were used in the Japan of the 1930s to that end. The Japanese, being thorough followers, could easily be persuaded once again that tourists taking pictures were spies looking for state secrets. The matter became a cause célèbre in 1984 when Stanislav Levchenko, a Soviet KGB major stationed in Japan, defected to the United States and told about his information-gathering activities. But the Japanese government has never been naive, and Soviet practices are known to be the same worldwide.

In the 1980s at least three rings of Japanese fishermen-spies traded "military secrets" to the Soviets at Sakhalin for permission to fish in the rich waters of Soviet territory. The system came unglued after the Soviets began to doubt the value of the "secrets" they were getting. The SDF had been aware all along of the exchange but had found it hardly worth the effort of stopping. So the Levchenko revelations had to be regarded as window dressing, not the cause of the LDP's new effort. Getting nearer to the root, the LDP members spoke of the growth of the Japanese Maritime Defense Force (navy) to a point where only three NATO countries had greater naval tonnage, and the growth of the Ground Defense Force (army) to a point where only four NATO powers had more than Japan's thirty-seven hundred armored vehicles, tanks and artillery pieces, and the growth of the Air Defense Force (air force) so that it stood fifteenth in the world of airpower. Actually in 1984 the Japanese did have military secrets, although legally they still had no army, navy or air force. (As noted, all members of the SDF are officially "civilians.") Further, Japanese defense industries had many technological secrets; the fact became common knowledge in 1984 thanks to the Americans pressing Japan for an exchange of high-tech information on defense affairs—an indication of American awareness of some militarily applicable aspects of Japanese superiority. The LDP wanted to protect the secrets. Also, the manner in which the law was framed indicated the potential emergence of a new military power: The draft legislation consisted of fourteen articles to protect defense and diplomatic secrets, classified information on foreign policy, diplomatic negotiations, secret codes and information on foreign countries. For a nation that had "renounced war and military force" this proposal was indeed strange.

7. "Kimigayo," the Japanese national anthem, means "Imperial Reign," and the song celebrates the rule of the emperor. Before and during World War II, schoolchildren first saw the Hinomaru— the rising sun flag—run up on the school flagpole, then sang "Kimigayo" before beginning classes. All this was a part of their worship of the emperor as the living symbol of Japan. The ceremony was much like the American pledge of allegiance, but after the surrender, "Kimigayo" fell into disuse, just as the national Japanese flag, the rising sun, was no longer flown from Japanese flagpoles.

In fact, as with the "demilitarization" of Japan, the social change was in part illusory. Some schools continued to raise the rising sun flag. Some schools continued to sing "Kimigayo."

The 1970s were marked by a new pride of citizenship. Japan had made her way up from the depths to the top again, and the Japanese knew it. By 1979 this new feeling of patriotism was beginning to make itself shown. One of the first incidents occurred in Fukuoka Prefecture. When the headmaster and teachers of Wakamatsu High School were preparing for the spring graduation ceremonies, what is known as the "Kimigayo" dispute broke out. The headmaster decided that this year the student body would show a little patriotic spirit. His decision was based on information from the national Ministry of Education noting that in 1982 they intended to push patriotism as a part of the national curriculum guidelines.

"Kimigayo," said the advance notice, was the national anthem, and singing it was going to be recommended. What the ministry was doing was again a part of the Japanese method of preparing the public for change. Such guidelines were and are far more important in Japan than any similar word that might come down in the United States from, say, the U.S. Department of Education. One of the results of the American occupation of Japan was the decentralization of control of the nation's educational system to follow the American pattern. But it never really did. The Ministry of Education curriculum guidelines had the practical effect of law. The number and sort of *kanji* (Chinese characters) taught to school children was "suggested" by the ministry, and the suggestion became the rule. Simplification of complex characters was made by the ministry and adopted by all Japan. The "Tokyo accent" and manner of speaking (Japanese as it is spoken over NHK, the national radio and television network) came down through the ministry to be the national guide.

The headmaster of Wakamatsu High School obviously agreed with the ministry that a little patriotism could be useful, and so even though all he had seen was a draft of a guideline to begin in 1982, three years earlier in 1979 he ordered the high school music instructor to prepare a version of "Kimigayo" for singing at the ceremonies.

The music teacher, a member of the Japan Teachers Union, had grown up detesting the song because of its "militarist connotations." Ordered to produce, he fabricated a jazzed-up version of the national anthem and played it on the piano at graduation. The audience was shocked, the headmaster got the teacher fired two months later, and the controversy began.

The Fukuoka Board of Education took up the cudgels for "Kimigayo," and headmasters were encouraged to use the patriotic song on ceremonial occasions: "The curriculum guideline says the song is the national anthem. It's natural that people sing it during school ceremonies. The real problem is that teachers are bringing the students and parents into the issue."

The teachers' unions fought on. And so after 1979 every spring graduation ceremony (March) and every enrollment ceremony for the new school year (April) was likely to become a donnybrook. One headmaster attended a faculty meeting shortly before graduation, ordered the song to be sung in the program and then skipped school until the day of the ceremony, fearful of personal reprisals by teachers. On another occasion, a vice-headmaster got up in the middle of the graduation ceremonies and instructed the students, faculty and parents to sing "Kimigayo."

The teachers' unions developed a methodology: *san nai toso*; three passive protests. They would not play the song, they would not sing it and they would not stand up, as was the custom, when it was being sung. The Fukuoka Prefecture Teachers Union, a part of the Japan Teachers Union, claimed that the forced singing infringed on the individual's right to choose his own thoughts and beliefs. Headmasters countered by taking the names of teachers and students who would not conform. Some students were encouraged by their teachers to join the protest. At one school located in the city of Kita Kyushu, a group sat down during the performance, then held a protest meeting and handed out posters and leaflets.

Despite this backlash, the popularity of "Kimigayo" continued to grow, and by 1984, at 105 of the 106 high schools in Fukuoka Prefecture, "Kimigayo" was sung at school functions. The practice spread across Japan. In the spring of 1984 the Osaka Board of Education heard a complaint from a local assemblyman that the headmaster of a municipal primary school had failed to teach "Kimigayo" to his pupils. Instead, he had been teaching them the songs of the North Korean People's Republic. This, said the assemblyman, was "ideologically prejudiced education policy." The

board found for the assemblyman. The principal was demoted to
the rank of ordinary teacher and transferred to the city educational
research office, and "Kimigayo" was taught properly thereafter.
So "Kimigayo," the national anthem of old, was making a very
strong comeback in Japan.

No one of these seven signs of change, by itself, meant that
militarism per se had returned to Japan. But taken together they
clearly indicated the return of a strong patriotic feeling, of nationalism, being instilled in children as it had not been for more
than thirty years. The whole atmosphere, and the public attitude
toward the Self-Defense Forces, was changing. The teachers were
among the first to sense the degree of change. In the spring of
1984 the Japan Teachers Union charged that the Self-Defense Forces
were making increasing attempts to promote the military image
among school pupils, particularly by distributing literature fea-
turing information about military life and weaponry to the junior
high schools.

In September the Nakasone cabinet issued its new defense white
paper, announcing that the Japanese people must be educated to
the need for a strong defense posture. Officially the government
said it was pursuing the program as a result of American pressure
to increase Japanese defense. Only partly true. The American insistence had opened a Pandora's box of doubt. More Japanese were
asking if they could, indeed, trust the Americans for defense in
time of trouble. The response of the government in its white paper
increased the level of concern, for the government reminded Japan
that the Soviets had increased their military presence in every way
in the area north of Japan and had two aircraft carriers scheduled
for the Pacific. The Soviet bases in Vietnam territory on Camranh
Bay gave the Soviets a strong position overlooking the Strait of
Malacca, which had once had two channels in its twenty-three-
mile width between Indonesia and Malaysia but now because of
silting had only one. Japan's access to the raw materials of Southeast Asia runs through the strait. None of this was now escaping
Prime Minister Nakasone's government, and the public was being

made increasingly aware of it every day.

Politically the matter of increased military attention and military buildup had to be managed by the government. The Liberal Democratic party, which had held power for most of the period since the beginning of the American occupation, had a record of promoting the military and nationalism. Some said the party was the home of the nascent militarists. Former Prime Minister Kakuei Tanaka, convicted of accepting bribes from America's Lockheed Aircraft Corporation while holding office, had been linked to the right wing of the LDP. His codefendant in the Lockheed case, who died in the winter of 1984, was Yoshio Kodama, widely known as an "ultranationalist," another term for militarist.

Kodama was a man of the military era. He was born in 1911 in a samurai family. During the Pacific War he organized a private intelligence agency called Kodama Kikan (Kodama Secret Service). He also operated a military procurement agency in China, from which he made millions. At the end of the war Kodama was found guilty as a class-A war criminal and went to Sugamo Prison. After he was released he went into politics as a silent partner, backing with money such politicians as prime ministers Ichiro Hatoyama and Nobusuke Kishi. He was also involved in various businesses and had relations with the underground criminal syndicates that run crime in Japan. He was a prime political fixer, and he was also organizer of Seishikai, an association of right-wing groups that in 1984 was reputed to number twenty-three organizations, though with only fifteen hundred acknowledged members.

Kodama finally got into trouble from his activities as "fixer." He was the secret agent of Lockheed International in Japan, and he presided over the bribery of Prime Minister Tanaka with billions of yen in connection with procurement of Lockheed military aircraft in the 1970s. Government forces uncovered the dealings, and Kodama and Tanaka and others were convicted and given prison terms.

The Lockheed scandal was reminiscent of some of the military procurement scandals of the 1920s and 1930s that hurt the image of political government and raised that of the military in Japan (even though it was a militarist politician involved). Notable was the easy victory won by former Prime Minister Tanaka to a fifteenth term in the Diet, *following his conviction*. The Tanaka political machine also managed to elect Tanaka's son-in-law, Naoki Tanaka, in Fukushima Prefecture. The machine was also helpful in other elections. The military, it seemed, could have it both ways—and only because this was the underlying sentiment.

By 1984, although all parties paid lip service to being against the Tojo era, the changes that were presaged indicated a growing response to the American demand for Japanese rearmament in a peculiarly Japanese fashion.

Prime Minister Nakasone and the LDP were working for "consensus" and not just on military affairs. They wanted a coalition era in Japanese politics, meaning broad national support for major changes in education, administration, diplomacy *and* defense. Japan was coming to the point of wanting change, wanting to cast off many of the Western ways forced on it by the U.S. in the late 1940s. The principal targets of the LDP for coalition were Komeito, the Soka Gakkai party; the Democratic Socialist party; and the New Liberal Club—all centrist organizations. Given enough strength, the government would then take the consensus as an invitation to speed up the changes.

The result was bound to be something more than the U.S. was looking for in the change of Japan's posture, unless the U.S. was willing to make some concessions in its approach to world affairs that seemed unlikely on the basis of the NATO experience in Europe: Japan would have to be taken in as a *full* partner in defense policy, at the planning level, which meant diplomatic as well as military.

Given the course of the American military urgings to the Japanese, a juggernaut was building in 1984 that was not likely to be stopped unless the U.S. somehow managed to convince an increasingly doubtful Japan that a serious long-term partnership was offered or in the offing. The political machinery was already spinning out national consensus for major, perhaps unintended by the U.S., changes in the future of Japan.

11
Articles of Faith

In old Japan religious institutions played a major role. In the days of the empire, and then the shogunate, warrior monks were enlisted by various political leaders to help in their struggles for power. From a modern point of view the most important Japanese development was the emergence of the Nichiren sect in the thirteenth century when the priest named Nichiren linked salvation to the lotus (*namu myoho renge kyo*—"reference to the wonderful law of the lotus"). He wanted Nichiren Buddhism to become the state religion of Japan, but he never achieved that ambition. After him, his followers maintained the same ambition. Nichiren Buddhism has always been linked with Japanese nationalism. From the days of the Meiji restoration in 1868, Shintoism was the state religion of Japan, but this native Japanese nature-faith was all-embracing and did not preclude, but made allowance for, an adherent's belief in another religion. Many of the army officers in the 1920s and 1930s professed the Nichiren faith, and when the army seriously began considering seizure of power in Japan in the 1920s, the generals did not ignore the religious organizations. In the 1920s there were some sixty Buddhist and twelve Shinto sects

137

in Japan, involving a quarter of a million temples and monasteries. The Nichiren, Tenro and Doin sects were particularly responsive to the military, and the Doin and Tenro were used to infiltrate Japanese influence into Korea, Manchuria, China, Mongolia and Taiwan. The Nichiren were closely allied with the young officers' groups that conducted terrorist activities in Japan in the 1920s and 1930s. Nichiren was particularly notable then for the Shanghai incident; in January of 1932 a number of Nichiren monks provoked a Chinese crowd in Shanghai and in the resulting fight several monks were killed. The Japanese military used the affair as an excuse to take control of part of Shanghai and then to demand economic and political concessions of extraterritoriality.

General Araki, one of the moving spirits behind Japanese imperialism and militarism, used the Nichiren sect for many purposes, not the least of which was control of the nation's youth. After the military seized control of all Japan, the government decreed that all students and all military personnel would attend divine service at Shinto chapels to cultivate "loyalty to the imperial house, love of country and a national spirit." To the students these orders were handed down through the central Ministry of Education.

The Nichiren Buddhists objected to this centralization, particularly since the Nichiren Buddhists had some ambitions of their own along that line. Tsunesaburo Makiguchi was an ardent Japanese nationalist at the turn of the twentieth century when Japan was seeking a new entity in the modern world, and he saw himself as the leader of a great organization that would make Japan an important power. He formed a lay group under the Nichiren umbrella called Nichiren Shoshu or Soka Gakkai that pursued a policy of expansion along with the Nichiren sect, always aimed at furthering Japanese nationalism.

By 1938 the Japanese had amalgamated the state with religion. Shinto, "the way of the gods," was thoroughly mixed into the political life of the nation, all centering around emperor worship. In the name of the emperor the military carried out their every act. The government held that Japan was one huge family of a single descent with the emperor as the nucleus, the emperor who came down in a direct line from the sun goddess herself.

By the middle of the 1930s the generals knew precisely where they were heading. How nicely Shinto fitted into their picture of the future, as drawn in a pamphlet put out in 1934 by the Ministry of War:

> War is the Father of Creation and the Mother of Culture. Rivalry for supremacy does for the state what struggling against adversity does for the individual. It is such impetus, in the one case, as in the other, that prompts the birth and development of Life and Cultural Creation.
>
> War, in this sense, does not conform to the generally accepted conception, in which it is held to consist of a series of terrific destructive acts perpetrated by massed people for unrelenting slaughter and devastation. War, thus characterized, is simply an inevitable outcome of the application of the idea that "might makes right" and an insatiable thirst for sheer conquests. Such definition of war must be rejected forthwith by our people, who have an unshakable faith in the all-pervasive Life of the Universe, and who are animated by the belief that it is their heaven-sent mission to participate in the great work of helping Life to unfold. To exalt war to such a high level is, in short, the mission of national defense.

Genchi Kato, a professor at Tokyo Imperial University, explained the Shinto belief for foreigners in 1935 this way:

> Shinto is not a religion *a posteriori* adopted purposely by the state as in the case of a state religion in a Western country, but the religion *a priori* of the heart and life of every Japanese subject, male or female, high and low, old and young, educated or illiterate. This is the reason why a Japanese never ceases to be a Shintoist, i.e., an inborn steadfast holder of the national faith, or one who embraces the national faith or the Way of the Gods as a group or folk religion as distinguished from a personal or individual religion, even though he may accept the tenets of

> Buddhism or Confucianism—probably Christianity here in Ja-
> pan is not excepted—as his personal or individual religion.

In other words, a Japanese was welcome to be anything he
wanted, so long as he was *also* a believer in the religion of the
people and the generals and the throne—Shinto.

As the 1930s proceeded, so did the stridence of the government
in raising Shinto to the pitch of fanaticism. The idea of the god-
nature of the emperor was one that had not ever really been pressed
even during the days of the shogunate. By 1940 the emperor's
deification was absolute, as it had never been even during feudal
days. The army had welded religion with the imperial system to
bring a unique power that destroyed the political party system and
left the power bloc of militarists in absolute control.

By 1941, using religion, education and the power of the media,
the militarists had convinced the Japanese people that they were
the superior race of the world, and therefore that they had a global
mission. Here is a statement by Yosuke Matsuoka, American-
educated foreign minister of Japan in the Tojo cabinet:

> I firmly believe that the great mission that Heaven has given
> to Japan is to save humanity in conformity with the great spirit
> in which Emperor Jimmu founded the Empire. Japan should
> take over the management of the continent (Asia) on a large
> scale, and propagate Hakko Ichiu and Kodo in Asia (the world
> under one roof, Japanese, and the Imperial Way) and then extend
> it to the world.

In 1941 the Great Nippon Young People's Organization (Dai
Nippon Seinen Kiko), which numbered virtually every schoolchild
and adolescent in Japan, held a contest for the most patriotic song.
Here is the winner, an embodiment of the "new Japan" created
by the generals in fifteen years (note: The Imperial Rescript refers
to the Imperial Rescript to Soldiers and Sailors, which by this time
had become so much a part of Japanese life that children in school
now memorized it):

We, the members of the Dai Nippon Young People's
    Organization,
Youth, fresh and new like the rising sun,
The Imperial benevolence sheds its radiance
    throughout the four corners of the earth,
Blue and clear is the sky
Blue and clear is the sky.
Looking up toward the flag of the Imperial
    Benevolence,
Let us arise with the Imperial Rescript in our hearts.

We, the members of the Dai Nippon Young People's
    Organization,
Leave on our destiny borne on strong wings.
Ah, where brilliant hope shines,
Strength and power prevails,
Strength and power prevails.
Bearing the future of our country on our
    shoulders,
We will live for the happiness of the
    people.

We, the members of the Dai Nippon Young People's
    Organization,
With fire burning in our steel-tempered bodies,
Ah, where sincerity pierces,
United in strong ties,
United in strong ties.
Treading on the thorny path,
We will realize the destiny of New Asia.

From there it was not hard to take the youth the rest of the
"Imperial Way." All nature was divine, everything that nature did
was also divine, and beyond good or evil. In the name of the
emperor, by 1939, Japan was called to make any sacrifice, or, as
the Department of Education explained the national policy, "to
give up one's life for the sake of the emperor cannot be called self-
sacrifice. It is rather discarding one's lesser self to live in the great
Imperial Virtue, and exalting one's true life as a national subject."

When late in 1941 the attack on the West came, the people of Japan were ready. The priesthood was ready. And in the spring of 1942 came the special spring festival at the Yasukuni Shrine for the deification of the war dead. Once more a poetry contest was staged, and the winning poem was printed in *Mainichi*, *Asahi*, *Yomiuri* and all other Japanese newspapers:

> In serving on the seas, be a corpse saturated with
>   water.
> In serving on land, be a corpse covered with weeds.
> In serving in the sky, be a corpse that challenges
>   clouds.
> Let us all die close by the side of our Sovereign,
>   without the slightest regret.

And so by 1941 the militarists had reached back within the deepest gloom and foreboding of the Japanese character to make of death a virtue. An extreme expression of this came from Captain Hideo Hiraide, a navy captain who spoke before a large Japanese crowd early in the Pacific War on patriotism:

"The passion of the samurai spirit is conveyed in the following stirring words: When you fall in action, see that you always face toward the enemy . . . Even after you have been beheaded in action, your bodiless head should fell one enemy by fastening itself on him by means of the teeth!"

Extreme, perhaps. But by 1942 virtually every Japanese who entered the military service expected death, and the family he left behind him had little illusion. This battle song won the first prize awarded by *Mainichi Shimbun* in the spring of 1942:

> Fall apart like the petals of a flower
> For the Emperor's sake.
> Fall apart and thus turn into a devil
> To protect our country.
> Three thousand years of glorious victory,
> Where ever our great army exists.

Such was the spirit of the militarism past. It engaged and over-whelmed an entire people to the point that at the end they very nearly were manipulated by the generals into a national mass attack on the Allied forces that was expected on the beaches, and that in the end, would have been followed by mass suicide of the sort that marked the end of the struggle for Saipan, when Japanese women and children threw themselves off the rocks at the upper end of the island rather than be captured.

There was another side to this preoccupation with death that was wrapped up with politics, patriotism and religion—an enor-mous ferocity, the darker side of *bushido*. I have found no better illustration of the horror than the account written by a Japanese enlisted sailor at Salamaua, New Guinea, of an incident in March, 1943, at the height of the battle for the South Pacific. The U.S. had conquered Guadalcanal. Admiral Yamamoto had been ordered by Imperial General Headquarters to capture southern New Guinea, including Port Moresby, and to hold in the Solomons, preparatory to recapturing Guadalcanal. The battle raged on land, on the sea and especially in the air. The Japanese were subjected to constant bombing, so strong and deadly that some broke under the strain. The feelings of the rest grew ever more intense.

Here is the diary entry of that Japanese sailor on New Guinea for March 29, 1943. A prisoner had been brought to the Japanese naval base at Salamaua, a captain who was a pilot and instructor in the American Army Air Force Transport Command at Port Moresby:

We all assembled at headquarters where one of the crew of a Douglas [C-47] shot down by antiaircraft March 18 was brought under guard.

Sub-Lieutenant Komai told us it had been decided to execute him and he was to be accorded a samurai's death.

We were assembled to witness the execution. The prisoner was given a drink of water outside the guardhouse. The chief surgeon, Lieutenant Komai, and a platoon commander bearing a sword, came from the officers' mess.

The time has come. The prisoner of war totters forward with his arms tied. His hair is cut loose.

I feel he suspects what is afoot, but he is more composed than I thought he would be. Without more ado he is put on a truck and taken to the place of execution.

The prisoner sits beside the chief surgeon and about ten guards accompany him. The noise of the engine echoes along the road in the hush of twilight. The sun has set and columns of clouds rise before us.

I glance at the prisoner and he seems prepared. He gazes at the grass, now at the mountains and sea.

At the execution ground, Lieutenant Komai faces the prisoner and says: "You are going to die. I am going to kill you with this Japanese sword according to the samurai code."

The lieutenant's face is stern. Now the time has come. The prisoner is made to sit on the edge of a water-filled bomb crater. The precaution is taken to surround him with guards.

When I put myself in his place the hate engendered by this daily bombing yields to ordinary human feelings.

The lieutenant draws his favorite sword, the famous Osamune [the Quieter]. The sight of the glittering blade sends cold shivers down the spine. First he touches the prisoner's neck lightly with the sword.

Then he raises it overhead. His arm muscles bulge. The prisoner closes his eyes for a second and at once the sword sweeps down.

Swish—it sounds at first like the noise of cutting, but is actually made by the blood spurting from the arteries as the body falls forward. Everybody steps forward as the head rolls on the ground.

The dark blood gushes from the trunk. All is over. There lies the head of a white doll.

I realize that the emotion I felt just now was not personal pity but a manifestation of the magnanimity that becomes a chivalrous samurai.

A superior seaman from the medical received the sword from the surgeon. He rolls the body on its back.

"Here's something for the other day—take that," he says, and with one sweep lays open the abdomen.

"These thickheaded white bastards are thick-bellied too," he remarks.

There's not a drop of blood left in the man's body. The seaman gives it a kick and then buries it.

The wind blows mournfully and the scene prints itself on my mind. Darkness descends.

In front of headquarters we got off the truck. If I ever get back alive, this will make a good story to tell. That's why I write it down.

But the unknown Japanese seaman did not get back alive. He was killed in the attack on Salamaua, and the diary was taken from his body.

He had died as he lived, under the Imperial Way of Shinto.

Small wonder that in the postwar occupation of Japan by the Americans, the state Shinto religion was outlawed. The question for the 1980s is: How dead is Shinto, and particularly the military manifestations of Shinto? That is a major reason for the attention focused on the status of the Yasukuni Shrine. That temple, above all others, is the symbol of the Japanese militarism of the 1930s and 1940s.

And even if in the 1980s one contends that the Shinto of the 1930s and 1940s is not reborn, one must reasonably consider what substitute may be waiting in the shadows of Mount Fuji.

With the changes that had to come Japanese ways of thinking about themselves and the rest of the world with the rearmament program, matters of the spirit would assume an importance unknown since the end of the Pacific War. Many in Japan deplore the inroads that Western materialism has made on their society even as they enjoy the benefits. But coming out from under the American umbrella, either as full partners, or eventually as independents and perhaps competitors, the materialism had to give way to a new spirit. The Self-Defense Forces, in particular, would have to have something spiritual to tie to—that is the Japanese way. Its precise form may not be altogether clear, but it must be strikingly similar to the old Japanese philosophical and religious institutions, including their ruthlessness with a military aspect and a chameleon's ability to roll with the times.

19 | Two-man submarine. This small submarine once lay at the bottom of Pearl Harbor. It was a part of the attack force on December 7, 1941. It was returned to Japan by the Americans and now rests in front of the museum at the Eta Jima academy.

20 | World War II antiaircraft gun. This gun and others like it are used to train Japanese Maritime Defense academy cadets in gun and ammunition handling as part of their officer candidate course.

21

22

23

21 | World War II two-man submarine.

22 | Japanese frigate in Eta Jima harbor.

23 | World War II naval guns. This battery is from the Japanese battleship *Mutsu* which was sunk in home waters at the end of the war.

24 | Japanese infantrymen on maneuvers. The Marston tracking is to keep tanks and wheeled vehicles from bogging down in the mud.

25 | Joint maneuvers with American troops in Hokkaido. The Japanese Self-Defense Force and American Pacific Defense Command forces train together regularly.

26 | Japanese infantryman on winter maneuvers in Hokkaido.
27 | Helicopter movement is a regular part of Japanese infantry training.

12

Japan in Search of Itself

*In my death see that a rash undertaking leaves
victory to chance and to the enemy. Accept the
Imperial Will faithfully, it will bring good fortune.*

*Remember that you are Japanese. You are the
treasure of the nation. With patience and the
determined spirit of the Special Attack Corps work
for the welfare of the Japanese people and for peace
in the world.*

> —Legacy of Vice-Admiral Takajiro,
> Onishi, developer of the Kamikaze
> Corps, to the youth of Japan,
> August, 1945, just before he
> committed *seppuku*

In the late 1940s and early 1950s Japan's sense of her own destiny
was decidedly askew. The presence of the victors as governors of
the land lay like a heavy blanket over the whole nation. The
unpleasantness of the occupation was relieved to a degree during
the Korean War, when it became apparent that the Americans
needed Japanese industry, and at the end of the war life began to
loosen up some for the Japanese.

In the 1950s and 1960s Japan worked hard to join the postwar
world, and in ten years began to produce remarkable goods. Japanese art shops opened in the larger American cities. Good ce-
ramics and pottery began to appear, as well as fine silks and cottons.
Soon Japanese department stores found it profitable to open
branches in a few American cities. Honolulu was a natural with
its large Japanese population. Shirokiya and Daei department stores
opened branches there and prospered. Takashimaya also opened
in New York on Fifth Avenue with considerable fanfare. And by

147

1960 Japanese goods, Japanese food and things Japanese were becoming favorably known in the culture centers of the United States. The really fine art, which had been known only to a few connoisseurs before, especially began to impress Americans.

At the same time Japanese manufacturers began making inroads in the higher technical fields, with radios, cameras and stereophonic systems that were at least as good as any manufactured in the world. Japanese optics, a well-kept secret before the war, blossomed into the Nikon and half a dozen other excellent brands of cameras. The Japanese also began producing what the Germans had developed and Detroit would not deign to notice: the small low-cost automobile. By the 1970s the Germans and Japanese shared most of that market, and only then did Detroit become upset enough to change.

By the 1980s, then, the Japanese had a good deal to be proud of, but the nation was still suffering from a vague apprehension that all was not as well as it might be, or might seem. Politically the country seemed to be settling toward a basically conservative coalition that would require give-and-take by the Liberal Democratic party and its middle-of-the-road partners. The Socialists and Communists would continue in opposition, with their only political chances resting on severe depression. By the winter of 1984–1985 the continued victory of conservative politicians perpetuated a semblance—and a sense—of stability that gave the LDP a feeling that they had a mandate.

Early in the 1980s the leaders realized that two generations had now come to maturity with no sense of the history or the traditions of the nation, and that in particular the glory that was the Japan of the early twentieth century had been wiped out by the American occupation and the heavy burden of guilt thrust on the Japanese. This recognition came at the same time that the U.S. was beginning to press hard for Japan to rearm and take a far greater role in the defense of the Pacific than the Japanese had envisioned.

Still, from the ashes of defeat, led by Premier Shigeru Yoshida in the earliest days, Japan had turned its energies from conquest to enterprise and trade and by the 1970s rivaled her American mentors in production and distribution. It is interesting to note the evaluation of this advance in a survey about Japanese pride conducted by the *Japan Times* in 1984 with a sample of 7,700 people. (More than one answer was permitted, which explains why the total percentage is over 100.)

THE PRIDE OF JAPAN

Reason	Percentage
The people's diligence and ability	33
The country's history and traditions	30
Natural beauty	28
Public order	24
Education	20
Culture and the arts	18
Humaneness	17
Science and technology	15
Social stability	15
Economic prosperity	14
Sense of duty	10
Unity of the people	4
No pride	14

Is the country headed in the right direction?

Yes	No	Don't know
26%	39%	35%

So here was a Japan in 1984 not responding to the issues as a Westerner might expect. National economic prosperity got only 14 percent as a source of pride as compared to overwhelming figures for pride in accomplishment, the national weal, the history and traditions. At the same time only 26 percent said the country was heading in the right direction.

What had developed was a new sort of pride in things *Japanese*, which *could* become the basis for the reestablishment of Japan as a major world power, a role she was being pushed toward by the United States. Until the 1980s, even with her growing industrial might and enrollment in the United Nations, Japan had maintained a low profile on the international scene. In Asia especially, and understandably, there was a nervousness as other nations remembered the Greater East Asia Co-Prosperity Sphere and other Japanese manifestations of imperialism in the 1940s. But fences were being mended in a quiet fashion. A visitor to the Philippines, who made the trip to Corregidor and spoke of the Bataan Death March, might be told by a Filipino guide that this tragic horror was "really perpetrated by Koreans," and while some Filipinos continued to express dislike of the Japanese, others said the Japanese years were really not so bad after all—proof of the conveniently erosive power of time on memory.

In official contacts the Japanese were careful not to offend Asian neighbors, nor to move to take any important leadership role in Asian affairs. But slowly with China, and then with the two Koreas, Japan began to make overtures for closer economic and social ties. By 1984 the Japanese and Chinese were talking openly of military matters; affairs went slower with South Korea, where the residue of hatred was greater. With North Korea, despite the usual fulminations of the Pyongyang publicity machine, Japan was opening the way for private Japanese traders to supply North Korea's hunger for manufactured goods and technology.

So, concomitant with the American demand for Japan to emerge from her American-imposed—but self-perpetuated—military lethargy, Japan was expanding her roles in the world.

Along with this came a realization by the government that national pride must be extended, and in the spring of 1984 the movement to secure the national consensus for this began when Dietman Motoharu Arima of the Liberal Democratic party from Kagoshima called for a celebration of the fiftieth anniversary of the death of Admiral Heihachiro Togo with these words:

"It seems that even the people of Kagoshima are beginning to forget who Admiral Togo was and that foreigners are more interested in him than the Japanese."

That call fell on responsive ground, and, as previously noted, the fiftieth anniversary celebration was duly held with an impressive list of foreign and Japanese guests. The memorial occasion was greeted by outcries from the Socialists that this was the opening of a campaign to restore militarism. They were right. The government was doing what the Socialists charged, and there was nothing the left wing could do about it.

The effort for consensus took various forms, orchestrated by various leaders and groups who had a stake in the restoration of military pride:

Item:–In April, 1984, the officials of the Yasukuni Shrine to the war dead enshrined 553 Nagasaki Medical College students who were killed in the atomic bombing of Nagasaki in 1945. They were the first civilians ever so enshrined at Yasukuni, and critics charged that this move (which occasioned a visit to the shrine by Prime Minister Nakasone) was part of the effort to restore the position of the Shinto religion in Japan.

Item:–Until 1983 most Japanese said little about World War II. Occasionally a survivor who had hidden out in the jungles of some remote island turned up, still doing his "duty to the emperor" until the last. But by the 1980s this phenomenon was running out; all the wartime soldiers were at least in their sixties then. It seemed unlikely by 1985 that there would be many more "hidden" survivors. Other than that reminder, the most frequent manifestations of Japanese interest in war history occurred in Hawaii, which had become a mecca for Japanese tourists and particularly honeymooners. Every day the tour boats from Honolulu set out, almost always bearing a group of Japanese passengers who came up to the U.S.S. *Arizona* Memorial at Ford Island and dropped flowers on the watery grave of the twelve hundred Americans who had perished aboard the battleship on December 7, 1941. This assuagement of Japanese national guilt had become a part of the Japanese presence in Hawaii.

But in 1983 a new element—one that might not have been acceptable earlier—was brought into the memorialization process. Six Imperial Japanese Navy veterans who had taken part in the

Pearl Harbor attack went to Hawaii to attend a memorial service on the forty-second anniversary of the attack. It was not, however, a mea culpa affair at all, but a service at a Nichiren Buddhist temple in honor of the *sixty-five Japanese who had been killed in the attack*. To be sure, the visitors also paid homage at the *Arizona* Memorial and the Punchbowl Memorial Cemetery to the fallen of the war. But the honoring of the Japanese at the site of what all Americans considered a dastardly sneak attack indicates how the followers of the Imperial Way had emerged from the shadows.

Item:—In the 1980s Japanese visited the Australian War Memorial Museum at Canberra, where a Japanese midget submarine was on display. The Australians had been most chivalrous in the treatment of the dead Japanese crews of the several submarines that penetrated Sydney harbor and were sunk there. The Japanese would come to visit the Tomb of the Unknown Soldier and leave flowers in memory of the war dead of both nations.

In the spring of 1984 a different sort of attention was being paid the memories of the Pacific War. At Yamaguchi, the directors of the Japan-U.S. Culture and Friendship Association began work to conserve a former Imperial Japanese Navy hangar at the Iwakuni Air Base and a number of Zero fighter planes that had escaped destruction when the Americans took over the base and simply left the planes alone. Most Japanese of the war-child generation had never seen a Zero fighter.

Item:—Also in 1984 four teams of representatives of the Japanese government set out for Truk, the wartime "Gibraltar of the Pacific," to collect the remains and personal effects of Japanese servicemen who had died aboard vessels sunk in Truk harbor. In the past there had been a few attempts to do some salvage work, some of it prompted by the Japanese Defense Agency's war historians, who had the difficult task in the postwar years of creating an official war history. So many of the Japanese records were lost during the war that the historians found themselves often relying on American accounts and records of the battles. But of the glory that was the Japanese military there was scarcely a trace. The *Yamato*, the largest battleship in the world, had gone down at Okinawa, sacrificed in the kamikaze spirit. The carriers, the army and navy aircraft were mostly all long gone. But by some Japanese definitely not forgotten. A motion picture company produced a film that in part glorified the *Yamato*, showing it miraculously restored and turned into a spaceship to participate in one of those Japanese films that really do seem to have been created in outer space. Of significance here was that the film showed the mighty *Yamato* steaming out on her way to her watery grave off Okinawa in that last kamikaze fling ordered by the navy. It was the first time that millions of Japanese had ever been given a view of their navy's superbattleship, the flagship of the storied Admiral Yamamoto. Japanese hearts were stirred.

Item:–In the spring of 1984 Nobuo Harada, a businessman who lived near Tokyo, came to the end of a ten-year search when he discovered a Mitsubishi type-O twin-engine bomber in the jungle on Yap, an island in what is now Northern Micronesia. This bomber, called the Betty by Americans, was one of Japan's most effective aircraft, used for transport, for high-level bombing and as a torpedo plane. At the end of the war all were destroyed. Not one remained in Japan. The plane found by Harada had crashed just after takeoff from a Yap airfield and was virtually intact. It was disassembled and brought back to Yokohama, where Harada planned to exhibit it in his personal museum.

All this activity was a part of a growing Japanese interest in the Pacific War and the old Japanese view of that war.

The left, among others, had been charging for years that the militarists had never been eliminated from Japanese society, that figuratively at least the attaché case of many Japanese businessmen contained samurai swords just waiting to be brandished. In the events of 1984 they had a real string to their bow. The spring and summer of 1984 were marked by innumerable events indicating a search by the government and its supporters for positive elements to reconstruct the military and social history of the old Japan of the Imperial Way.

Indeed, even the Socialist party began to feel the pressure for a new approach to things military. For years Party Chairman Masashi Ishibashi had held that the Self-Defense Forces law was unconstitutional. The party announced in a two-day convention in March, 1984, that it stood for Japanese neutrality and that Prime Minister Nakasone's call for a drastic review of postwar government policies inherited from the occupation days was a plot to lead Japan into rewriting the constitution and becoming a military power once again. But finally Ishibashi "clarified" his position. The SDF, he said, "is a legal entity created under an unconstitutional law." This clarification (hedging) left the Socialist supporters and Socialists' friends more confused than ever, but most dissenters decided not to press the Socialist chairman any further, and thus Chairman Ishibashi was able to enjoy that very Japanese position of being simultaneously against and not against something—in this case, the SDF.

Chairman Ishibashi became, it seems, a realist. He visited the United States in April, 1984, and made the party's peace with the U.S. for the first time. He announced that the class war was not really necessary after all. Armed with this disarming statement for the capitalists, Ishibashi visited various U.S. officials. Japan's ties with the United States, he said, had to be closest of all. This was news, since the Socialist party had led in attempts to sever those ties for twenty years.

Still, Ishibashi did all this without sacrificing the party's opposition to the U.S.-Japan military alliance or to what he saw as reviving Japanese militarism. His explanation to the Americans was that they did not understand the strength of nationalism and militaristic sentiments in Japan. Democracy in Japan, he said, was not yet firmly established, and his implication was clear: The Liberal Democratic party, which had controlled Japanese politics almost steadily for forty years, had to be suspected of promoting militarism in Japan.

A basic change in the Japanese attitude toward defense appeared early in 1984: the end of the government's head-in-the-sand policy toward American movement in Japanese waters with atomic weapons. The change was occasioned by an article that appeared in the U.S. secretary of the navy's annual report. It indicated that since 1960 American vessels had been traveling to Japan and back carrying nuclear weapons. This had been suspected but officially denied by the Japanese government. But here it was in black-and-white, as discovered by the Kyodo news agency, which now printed the names and dates on which submarines had come to Japan with nuclear devices. The news was front-page headline material all over Japan. One of the first vessels was the *Grayback*. All the details were there: travel in Japanese waters from March 12 to May 17 continuously, carrying nuclear warheads, Regulus II missiles, which she had brought from Hawaii. The long story also detailed the "war patrols" of the *Grayback*, which took it into Makassar Strait and other areas—and all this while the Japanese and American governments flatly denied such activity.

By the summer of 1984 it had become a recognized fact in Japan that U.S. atomic weapons were coming in and out of Japanese waters, and the consensus was beginning to work here as well. Theoretically, the Japanese were to be consulted each time a nuclear weapon approached; in fact, it did not matter. The Japanese cabinet was able to say that *policy* had not changed, and in this way to pass off the issue. That the antinuclear forces in Japan were able to make no more fuss than they did, and have no more influence than they did, was an indication of the way the wind was blowing.

In the spring several groups protested against new deployment of American vessels in Japanese waters. The nonnuclear submarine *Barbel* was sent to Sasebo, and the Japanese antinukes charged that the reason was to monitor Soviet nuclear submarines. They further claimed that atomic-missile-bearing submarines were to be brought in. The government scarcely flinched, and whatever the combined sea forces of Japan and the United States were up to, they did not stop.

In August, Tokyo was the site of a ban-the-bomb conference, which brought foreign representatives as well as Japanese. Some six hundred people met to condemn the bringing of nuclear weapons to Japan and to express concern over the danger of the U.S.-

Japan military alliance and growing Japanese rearmament. They talked about "alternative defense," which meant a national defense without armed services—apparently a variation on Gandhi's passive resistance. The protesters were joined by others to march in a huge peace rally in Tokyo's Hibiya Park and through the streets by lantern light. The net effect on the Japanese military buildup was zero.

The way in which the wind was blowing over Tokyo was also shown in August, 1984—traditionally since 1945 August was the month in which the pacifists gathered in Japan to lament the use of the atomic bomb at Nagasaki and Hiroshima, and to speak against the Self-Defense Forces, the Japan-America defense treaty and nuclear weapons in general. In 1984 the meetings were fragmented. The Japan Congress Against Atomic and Hydrogen Bombs (Gensuikin), formed by the Japan Socialist party, and the Japan Council Against Atomic and Hydrogen Bombs (Gensuikyo), formed by the Japan Communist party, had been meeting together for several years. In 1984 the meeting very nearly came unstuck over the issue of American submarines and Tomahawk missiles with their atomic warheads. The Gensuikin was even inclined to favor the U.S.-Japan security alliance, while still opposing atomic weapons. Even there the hard line of the past was softening, a process spurred on by Soviet deployment of at least one hundred thirty triple-headed SAS-20 missiles, which were clearly facing Japan and China. Polls showed that the Japanese people, who were very much aware of the Soviet military buildup in Sakhalin and in the four Soviet-held islands above Hokkaido that Japan still claimed, favored the U.S. treaty although the work on the consensus to favor atomic weapons had not yet begun. Still, it was significant that in the fall of 1984 the question of Japan's nuclear potential kept coming up, and the nation was assured by the scientists and politicians that Japan had the capability, and could produce nuclear weapons very quickly if it ever wanted to.

But, of course, nobody wanted to.

13

The New Industrial Power

The old-fashioned call it *zaibatsu*. The moderns call it *zaikai*. Whatever the name, it represents the continuation of the nineteenth- and twentieth-century Japanese industrial combinations of great power that brought Japan first into the Western world, then supported its military through the Pacific War, and never died, although lip service was paid to the story that the concentration of Japanese capital in the hands of a few powerful combines was wiped out in 1946.

One needs to understand what Japan had before the surrender to the Allies in order to evaluate where it is in the 1980s and where it may be going.

Under the shogunate, Japan's important families warred, and their satellite lords fought with them. By the fifteenth century some three hundred feudal lords struggled for power and out of this struggle came the *daimyo* system, the *daimyo* being warlords within their own boundaries.

The *daimyo* and their samurai suffered constant cash flow problems, and the principal sources of money were the traders who dealt in rice and other necessities. In the sixteenth century, with a Japanese population of twenty million people, Japan's gross national product could be stated as 1.17 billion kilograms of rice. The names of the traders Mitsui and Sumitomo were already known as those of men with ready cash. At the end of the sixteenth century the Sumitomos created Japan's first bank. Soon a third important trading clan made its appearance: Mitsubishi, a trading firm founded by a prince of the Tosa clan.

With the emergence of the Tokugawa shogunate economic power was concentrated in fewer hands. The shogun controlled all. An important *daimyo* might be granted an income of 180 million kilograms of rice, but for this he had to maintain twenty-five thousand samurai to fight for the shogun. And each of those samurai had a position to maintain. Further, the samurai were forbidden by the shogunate to engage in farming, crafts or trade. By the middle of the nineteenth century this system had broken down and some samurai had become *goshi*, or village samurai. They tilled the fields; they also became millers and distillers and large landowners. Also some peasants became wealthy men (*gono*).

With the opening of Japan to trade and visitations by Westerners, industrialization speeded up. The fortunate moneyed class secured monopolies from the government. Mitsubishi, for example, was granted a monopoly on shipping lines and the right to levy its freight charges in silver so regardless of what happened to the yen in the marketplace Mitsubishi prospered. The capital for expansion was also found in the hands of the wealthy farmers who had now largely forsaken the land to become businessmen. Emperor Meiji in 1868 began, as mentioned, the building of a Japan along modern Western industrial lines. By 1900 the number of industrial workers had risen to 338,000. Fifteen years later there were more than a million. Industry had by this time risen to a value of ¥2 billion, or about 40 percent of the total Japanese gross national product.

The Russo-Japanese War created many fortunes, including those of Asano, Okura and Yasuda. The Kuhara family received a monopoly to supply ore for the government steel plants at Yawata. Mitsui lent money to the Wada and Muto families, who took over the Japanese textile industry. But Mitsui, of course, had a piece of it.

As Japan expanded militarily the big money combines moved right in with the troops. Mitsui, Mitsubishi, Sumitomo and Kuhara all had their investments in Manchuria and Korea—in 1903 they had invested ¥888 million. By 1908, following the Japanese victory in the Russo-Japanese War, the industrial investment had risen to ¥1.2 billion. The South Manchurian Railway Company was a part of this combine, owning steel mills, coal mines, iron ore mines, shipyards, machine tool factories and all manner of industrial firms.

After World War I, Japan felt the brunt of depression. The artificial demand for manufacturers generated by the war ceased, and as unemployment grew, Japan was hit by strikes and riots over rice. The solution to the economic difficulties appeared to the industrialists to be creation of new markets. They had already expanded into Taiwan, Korea and Manchuria, and despite the bad times at home the investors were making profits in these areas. A survey of Japanese industry in 1927 found that light industry predominated, which meant the big industrial combines were more interested in producing for sale to the people and to China and other countries rather than in building up the industrial potential and the self-sufficiency of Japan. The generals and admirals, who were beginning to look for expansion of their power, not surprisingly objected to the direction of the *zaibatsu*, and the younger or "progressive" elements of the army reviled the industrialists as part of the enemy forces that were preventing the establishment of "the new Japan." To tempt the *zaibatsu* and secure their support, the military in 1928 submitted a plan to the government for promotion of key industries, "increasing state subsidies to war-industry firms and industries that will play a premier role in the event of war."

The industrialists saw the handwriting on the wall, and began to fall in line behind the military. By 1930 the Yawata steel mills were producing 62 percent of the output of steel for the army and navy, and two thousand factories were working on military orders.

War production became the mainstay of the big monopoly groups during the world depression that followed the New York and London stock market crashes. Mitsui and Mitsubishi had ¥250 million invested in war industry. Matsukata had ¥90 million, Kuhara ¥80 million.

In order to stimulate war production these and other firms were given fat government contracts and outright subsidies. By 1931 Mitsubishi and others had built eight aircraft factories and six aircraft-engine factories, each subsidized by the government. The army and the navy insisted that Japan must be self-sufficient in every way, so optical factories were built modeled on the best of the Germans', as well as radio, telephone, metallurgical, acid, rubber—every sort of factory that could produce the needs of the military was erected, and the government paid. Obviously, the well-being of the big industrial combines depended on the well-being and goodwill of the military. For years Mitsui, Mitsubishi and the other industrial firms had played politics with one party or the other. But in the 1930s the young militarists lost all patience with any politician who stood in their way, and pressed the industrial combines so that they threw their political weight behind the army and navy demands on the civil government.

By 1931 Japan had seven million factory workers, in factories built with government assistance of ¥4 billion. The private capital in these industries was only ¥8.5 billion; in other words the government subsidies amounted to nearly half of the capital. The term *zaibatsu* certainly filled the combination of big companies—*zai* for the character meaning money or wealth, *batsu* meaning a combine.

To impress the Chinese and other Asians the Japanese set up Manchuria as the puppet state Manchukuo, or "Manchu nation." Pu Yi, the last of the Manchu dynasty, had been wrenched from a pleasant life in north China to become a puppet ruler. It had a constitution, a cabinet, a judicial system; its own police, army, foreign ministry and all the trappings of state. But it was controlled absolutely by the Japanese, and the real ruler of Manchukuo was the commander of the Kwantung Army. The decisions announced by the Manchurians were made by the fifty-three hundred Japanese "advisors" to the government, most of them Japanese army officers. The development and exploitation of Manchurian resources and industry were carried out by the *zaibatsu* as an integral part of the Japanese economy.

Spurred by the profit motive, the *zaibatsu* did a good job for the Japanese militarists in building up the industrial capacities of Japan and the conquered territories, but there were still problems for the generals and admirals. In 1937 after the Japanese had invaded China and moved into territory where two hundred million Chinese lived, the government in Tokyo became nervous over the continued military adventures of the generals in China and Manchuria. The bitter joke going around Tokyo was that Japan had two military organizations: the army and navy general staffs in Tokyo, which were responsive to the emperor's wishes and the prime minister's government, and the army and navy in China and Manchuria, which were out of control. It was true: The ultranationalistic generals and admirals of the "new Japan" rode roughshod over their conservative compatriots and ignored or bullied the civilian cabinet into submission. Virtually all that happened in the late 1930s tended toward militarist control of Japan. One of the leading militarists, General Araki, wrote a paper that explained the policy of the militant generals and admirals, "Japan's Mission in the Showa Era":

"The capitalists are merely concerned with their own interests, paying no attention to the life of society; politicians frequently forget the overall situation in the country, caring only for the interests of their party . . . the state is above classes and party interests. It protects the interest of the nation as a whole. For that reason it must be given the final say on matters affecting the life of society."

For "state" one may read "army."

By 1940 the *zaibatsu* had come into line behind the army, and thereby had gained sufficient power in the government apparatus largely to control national economic policy. As the army bullied its way into power, the war in China was extended until the war party of the military was in so deep that it could not extract itself.

The ultimate step was the invasion of Indochina, which alerted the Western world to Japan's intentions to conquer Asia. By this time the Japanese army in China could not withdraw without losing face abroad and at home; by that time the United States would accept nothing less than Japanese withdrawal from China. And in 1941 the *zaibatsu* had hitched its star to the militarists. The army gave up all pretense of working through the civil government and took over. The result was the choice of a new military prime minister, General Hideki Tojo, a member of the war party. On January 27, 1941, Tojo issued his plan for the Greater East Asia Co-Prosperity Sphere, which called for the Japanese takeover of the Soviet Union's Siberian maritime regions. The militarists, in control of all Japan before December 7, 1941, soon did away with political government altogether. Political parties were outlawed and replaced by the Imperial Rule Assistance Association, which consisted of the men the militarists wanted in their government.

As for the *zaibatsu*, these huge trusts completely dominated the Japanese economy. They allocated markets, fixed prices and after 1940 joined with the army in dictating national policies. During the war they not only prospered in Asia; they traded with neutral and Axis countries as well, making enormous profits. They were recognized by the Allies as the key to the Japanese economy, and in 1945 one of General MacArthur's earliest pronouncements was that he was dissolving the *zaibatsu*.

At the time of surrender the caretaker government of Prince Higashikuni had turned over some ¥40 million to the big industrial firms, payments on war contracts that would never be completed—an act that was nothing less than a raid on the national treasury to enable the *zaibatsu* to stash away money in the face of defeat.

In fact, the American occupation was less than onerous. General MacArthur, as mentioned, chose to deal through the Japanese government. The establishment of the Supreme Command for the Allied Powers took some considerable management, including the cooperation of men such as those who directed the *zaibatsu*. And by the time the plans were made to break up the *zaibatsu*, the international political situation had changed significantly. Originally Washington had also insisted that Japan be demobilized and the *zaibatsu* be destroyed, but by the winter of 1946 it had become apparent that U.S.-Soviet relations were already deteriorating. American military and diplomatic leaders began rethinking the exigent wartime policy of Soviet-American cooperation. By spring, a Soviet-American impasse had developed over the reunification of Korea, and it was apparent there would be two Koreas. China was in revolution, as was Indochina. The communists threatened to seize control in Malaya and the Philippines. One American military administrator in Japan predicted to newspaper correspondent Mark Gayn that Japan would eventually be an American ally in the struggle with the USSR. "Let's not kid ourselves," he said. "We need a strong Japan, because one of these days we'll have to face Russia and we'll need an ally [in the Pacific]. Japan is it."

The *zaibatsu* did, of course, suffer some serious blows. They lost their investments in Manchuria, Korea and Taiwan. In Manchuria the Soviets stripped whole factories to the ground, though they could not uproot the hydroelectric facilities or such great pits of natural resources as the Anshan coal mines. The Koreans, of the north and south, took over whatever the Japanese had built there, although the North Koreans were subjected to some heavy Soviet withdrawals they could not protest. Except for Taiwan, which became a windfall for the Chiang Kai-shek government, there was very little Japanese investment elsewhere in the Greater East Asia Co-Prosperity Sphere.

But as the political dissolution of the old Asia continued, and the new realignments of power among the ex-Allies began to emerge, it was increasingly perceived that the destruction of the *zaibatsu* would not assist American policy in Asia. And in fact the plan to break up the *zaibatsu* firms and sell their shares never got off paper. Only seventeen war plants were dismantled and sent to Britain, China and the Philippines. It was decided in Tokyo and Washington that the USSR had done very well by itself in Manchuria and North Korea and was entitled to nothing more. In 1946 and 1947 the experts studied the question of reparations, a study that was nothing more than a stall. They had already decided nothing was going to happen. With communist power growing in the countries around Japan and a socialist government squeaking into power in Japan, the U.S. took another look at what it was accomplishing. Socialist Prime Minister Tetsu Katayama seemed to pose a serious threat. The SCAP-designed destruction of the old order threatened, many felt, to send Japan to socialism if not communism before it was finished.

By 1948 any visible amity between the Western and Eastern blocs had disappeared, and what Winston Churchill termed "the cold war" had broken out. The U.S. renounced reparations, and SCAP said there would be no further disruption of the Japanese economy. In the same year President Truman sent General MacArthur a new nine-point economic stabilization program for Japan that put an end to pressure on the *zaibatsu*. Joseph M. Dodge, a Detroit banker who had supervised the reform of currency and the economic system of West Germany, came to Tokyo to oversee the American effort to revitalize a Japan it had spilled its blood to defeat. Instead of taking away, the conqueror gave. The Japanese were granted American credits and assisted in finding in Southeast Asia and elsewhere the markets they had lost in Korea, Manchuria and China. And as Japan began to prosper her companies also invested money in Taiwan, South Korea, Thailand and Indonesia. In September of 1951 the treaty between the United States and Japan was signed, and a year later American occupation forces were totally withdrawn from Japan; after that Americans in Japan were "guests" living on bases leased from the Japanese. The next year, 1953, the Diet revised the laws covering the *zaibatsu* and in the next thirty years passed forty new laws that encouraged cartelism—all without a single complaint from the United States.

Even before this time, Japanese industry had been turned back to war production, for the use of the United Nations forces fighting in Korea. The firms that were providing the war matériel? Shin Mitsubishi Jukogyo (New Mitsubishi Heavy Industries); Kawasaki Kokuku (Kawasaki Aircraft); Osaka Kinzoku (Osaka Metal

Industry); Kondo Seiko (Kondo Steelworks); Komatsu Seisakusho (Komatsu Manufacturing Division) and so forth. All had been Japanese war industries. All were part of the new *zaikai*, the old *zaibatsu* in a new kimono. In all, nearly two hundred fifty Japanese companies turned their efforts to the supply of the American war effort in Korea.

Japan's war industries proceeded to prosper enormously and grow prodigiously. They supplied the Japanese Self-Defense Forces: artillery, tanks, aircraft, small arms, ships. Some of these matériels were manufactured under American licenses, including the Nike ballistic missile capable of carrying an atomic warhead, but Japan was back in the position achieved by the militarists in the late 1930s. Physically, it was and is ready once again to become a great military power. Mitsubishi, for example, which had built perhaps 20 percent of Japan's war matériel in the 1940s, now in the 1980s is building about 30 percent of Japan's war matériel, from aircraft and warships to electronics. And within the *zaikai* system, tight control has again become the way of business.

In 1964 Shin Mitsubishi Jukogyo, Mitsubishi Nihon Jukogyo (Mitsubishi Japan Heavy Industries) and Mitsubishi Zosen (Mitsubishi Shipbuilding) merged to become the largest heavy engineering and war production firm in Japan. A new trust. In the 1970s other *zaikai* firms got together to form enormous trusts, such as Kawasaki's railroad car, aircraft and heavy engineering firms merging to become Kawasaki Jukogyo (Kawasaki Heavy Industries). Yawata Seitetsu and Fuji Seitetsu merged to become Shin Nihon Seitetsu, or New Japan Iron Works, the largest steel trust in the world. And all this was accomplished in some twenty years. The reason it could be done, of course, was that Japanese industry had never been destroyed as the people of the Allied nations believed. Much hoopla about the B-29 firebomb raids had been passed off in the media as fact. If a steel mill was bombed and some essential area of it was hit, production might stop, but that did not mean the steel mill itself was destroyed. In spite of all the talk about destruction of Japanese industry during the war, the Japanese generals were right when they said Japan could still fight as of August, 1945. Its most serious problem was the cutoff of oil from the East Indies. The enemy's submarines had interdicted the fuel supply, and the Japanese had been forced to turn to artificial oil made from pine trees. There was fuel in the tanks but in limited supply, being hoarded by the military for the last great battle for Japan itself.

The Japanese industrial recovery—"the economic miracle"—was not a miracle at all. America backed it financially and provided the supplies. The losses suffered by Japan through air raids on its islands had surely been high in terms of housing and population but industrially it was not badly off. In August of 1945 steel, heavy engineering and chemical industries were operating at 50 percent above the 1937 level. The aluminum industry (aircraft) was six times as big as it had been in 1937. The real problem of the old *zaibatsu*, once it had adjusted to the loss of plants in Korea, Manchuria and Taiwan, was technological. The war had brought enormous technological advance to the United States, Britain and even Germany while Japan had to sacrifice research and advance to keep its industry alive. Peace brought all this modern technology to Japan free of charge when the U.S. decided to rebuild the Japanese economy. The Japanese were encouraged to lean heavily on the Americans after 1950 for technology; in the next twenty years Japan bought twelve thousand licenses for use of various foreign products and procedures. In those years it made good use of what it licensed. Rapid growth also benefited from a new feeling of challenge in Japan. Japanese workers, trained in war to "cooperate," continued in that mode; unlike the American system of labor-management confrontation, the Japanese followed a highly developed and structured form of cooperation that paid off in terms of productivity. In the years 1950–1970, while American productivity rose at the rate of 4 percent and Britain's rose at 3 percent, Japan's rate of growth was 15 percent. By 1970 Japan had risen to second place in the world as industrial producers, leading the world in the building of ships, cameras, radio sets, television, and was a major competitor for trade in pig iron, steel, autos, acids, plastics, synthetic rubber and chemicals.

In the 1980s Japan had moved apace in the "high-technology" field. In 1984 it was beginning to challenge American predominance in computers and other aspects of the "information revolution." Matsushita Electric Industrial Company became the nation's biggest money earner in 1979 and stayed that way for the next four years. In 1983 the company earned over $2 billion in profits. Toyota Motor Company was second with just under $2 billion. But, of course, those were *individual* companies. *Zaibatsu* figures were concealed. Suffice it to say that Mitsui and Mitsubishi cartels' consolidated sales each came to more than ¥66 billion.

One might think that with this sort of business success the *zaibatsu* would relax. Not so. In the fall of 1984 a government advisory body recommended to the cabinet a five-day work week of forty-five hours, which would mean a considerable increase over the average Japanese workweek of 41.7 hours. Obviously the *zaibatsu* was behind this plan. The proposal was typically Japanese, announcing that the increased workweek would be a "transitory step toward shorter working hours." Longer was shorter!

Labor unions took violent exception, but the idea did not die. If it survives, if it becomes the law of the land, that would mark a big step on the way to state control of industry, and a look back at what happened in the 1930s should indicate the danger: The militarists could never have moved and created a war economy had they not gained control of industry.

In the 1980s Japan's *zaikai*, or new *zaibatsu*, number six groups. Mitsubishi, Mitsui, Sumitomo, Dai Ichi Bank, Fuji Bank and Sanwa Bank. In the new world of finance their central structure of authority is built around banking and insurance. But all else is there too. With their tentacles, each is a major element of Japanese industry:

MITSUBISHI

Mitsubishi Bank
Mitsubishi Trust Company
Meiji Life Insurance Company
Tokyo Marine Insurance Company

Mitsubishi Mining Company
Mitsubishi Copper Company
Mitsubishi Metal Company
Mitsubishi Electric Company
Mitsubishi Chemical Company
Edokawa Chemical Company
Mitsubishi Glass Company
Mitsubishi Oil Company
Mitsubishi Paper Company
Mitsubishi Trading Company
Mitsubishi Warehouse Company
Mitsubishi Land Company

MITSUI

Mitsui Bank
Mitsui Trust Company
Mitsui Life Insurance Company
Mitsui Mining Company
Mitsui Metal Company
Mitsui Shipbuilding Company
Mitsui Chemical Company
Mitsui Trading Company
Mitsui Real Estate Company
Mitsui Warehouse Company
Mitsui Shipping Company
Mistui Construction Company
Mitsui Agriculture Forestry Company
Osaka Shipping Company
Showa Aircraft Company
Japan Flour Mills
Tokyo Cotton Company
Plus a dozen smaller companies

SUMITOMO

Sumitomo Bank
Sumitomo Trust Company
Sumitomo Life Insurance Company
Sumitomo Marine Insurance Company
Sumitomo Coal Company

Sumitomo Mining Company
Sumitomo Cement Company
Sumitomo Metal Company
Sumitomo Electric Company
Sumitomo Chemical Company
Sumitomo Machinery Company
Sumitomo Trading Company
Sumitomo Warehouse Company
Sumitomo Real Estate Company
Plus twenty or thirty small companies

DAI ICHI BANK

Dai Ichi Bank
Asahi Life Insurance Company
Furukawa Mining Company
Furukawa Electric Company
Yokohawa Rubber Company
Fujio Electric Company
Nippon Light Metal Company
Kawajaki Heavy Chemical Company
Kawajaki Steel Company
Kawajaki Electric Company
Kawajaki Shipping Company
Kawajaki Aircraft Company
Plus others

FUJI BANK

Fuji Bank
Yasuda Trust Company
Yasuda Life Insurance Company
Yasuda Fire Insurance Company
Oki Electric Company
Kokusaku Pulp Company
Showa Electric Company
Showa Shipping Company
Nissan Automobile Company (Datsun)
Japan Airline Company
Japan Refrigeration Company
Japan Cement Company

Hitachi Manufacturing Company
Tokyo Construction Company
Tokyo-Yokohama Railway Company
Plus others

SANWA BANK

Sanwa Bank
Toyo Trust Company
Japan Life Insurance Company
Nippon Rayon Company
Nippon Textile Company
Teijin Textile Company
Kansai Paint Company
Osaka Cement Company
Nakayama Copper Company
Hidachi Manufacturing Company
Marujen Oil Company
Hidachi Shipbuilding Company
Toyomo Rubber Company
Nippon Transportation Company
Takashimaya Department Store Company
Plus others

These new *zaikai* are to the old *zaibatsu* as bullet trains are to palanquins. A look at the names of their companies shows the manner in which they control: Mitsubishi management has an idea for a new industry, the bank finances with the help of the trust company, the insurance companies insure, the raw materials come up the company line, they are shipped in company ships and delivered to company warehouses, a new factory is bought through Mitsubishi Land Company and gets it technology from Mitsubishi industries . . . a combine such as Mitsubishi is as large and powerful as the total industrial plant of some entire countries. And don't forget there are six such superpower cartels in Japan.

Were that not staggering enough, where the supergiants find competition hurtful, they combine, as in New Nippon Steel Company, which is controlled by the supercartel of the six new *zaikai-*

zaibatsu. Tokyo Electric is another instance; to avoid competition Mitsubishi and Mitsui combined to control that company. New Nippon Steel is the result of mergers to which Fuji Bank and Mitsubishi decided to contribute rather than to compete with.

The old *zaibatsu* consisted of three major groups. The *zaikai* has had three new ones added. Further, all now work under banking control; the banks, in turn, are financed by the Bank of Japan, the central bank of the nation, from which the private banks borrow constantly at extremely low rates of interest to support their industrial operations.

Control is exercised by the major figures in these six cartels, working with government officials. Nippon Kogyo, the Japanese Industrial Club, is the place where most of the big decisions are made.

There was still one catch to all this activity in 1984. Japanese capitalism, largely spawned by American capitalism, was seen by elements of American industry as being naturally subservient to it. American business complained that the Japanese did not allow sufficient competition by foreign business firms within Japan— and such "Japan-bashing" has become a new and growing preoccupation.

"The objective is to fabricate 'facts' and use them to demonstrate how Japan's international trade policies create economic disruption that warrants retaliation," writes Johns Hopkins University Professor Steve H. Hanke. For example:

The "fact": Japan's markets are closed to American exports while American markets are open to Japan.

The reality: The tariffs of Japan, along with Switzerland and Sweden, are the lowest in the world. For all nonagricultural industries Japan's tariff average rate is 36 percent lower than that for the same industries in the United States. Its highest rates are on twenty agricultural products. Even these are low by international standards. Japan is the largest foreign market for U.S. limes, lemons, grapefruit, sorghum, beef, pork and chicken, and the second largest market for American soybeans and wheat.

The "fact": Japan controls imports by strict quotas.

The reality: By international standards Japan has one of the best records for elimination of quotas on foreign imports. Since the 1960s Japan has reduced the number of items covered by quota by 85 percent.

The "fact": When Japan is unable to prevent import by tariff or quota, it uses bureaucratic restrictions and ties up the exporter in red tape.

The reality: Japan is an adherent to the General Agreement on Tariffs and Trade's standards code. This code controls the discrimination against imports; the GATT has well-defined procedures to cover complaints. There have never been any complaints to that body against Japan.

Despite the plaints (particularly from the American automotive industry and automotive labor), the reality, says economist Hanke, is that Japan does not often employ such barriers, and when it does its restrictions are much less than those of the United States and the European Common Market.

So what might be the real reason for Japan-bashing? The uncomfortable truth seems to be that it has stemmed from American business' and government's belief that Japan could be pushed into turning around the American trade deficit because Japan, in 1984, was still in many ways a dependent of the United States. Certainly this has been the view in Tokyo.

As of the 1980s, eighty-three of the two hundred major American corporations are operating in Japan: Twelve of twenty-three major electrical firms; eleven of twenty American petroleum companies; ten of sixteen major American chemical companies; six of seven major American pharmaceutical companies. The percentage of business is enormous: American petroleum firms control more than half the Japanese market.

This U.S. presence has been used by the Japanese industrialists as an excuse to merge and merge, creating ever larger monopolies. As in the 1930s, the official policy has been to support the monopoly system. If the *zaikai-zaibatsu* needed an excuse for the growing centralization of economic power, they have had it in the constant American business pressure to take over Japanese markets. And, of course, a centralized economy is always a temptation to those powerful enough to take it over—such as the militarists.

Most publicized in the U.S. has been the supposedly unfair competition from Japan in the automobile area. But Japan had no tariff on foreign cars. The Japanese prefer their own autos, and Japanese and many Americans prefer the price, size and quality of the Japanese product, which has generally been cheaper, smaller and better than Detroit's. The Japanese have made concession after concession, limiting their shipment of autos and going into joint ventures with American auto firms in America, at times using labor they considered inferior in order to placate the American labor movement. They made more concessions than any industry anywhere has ever made to a foreign government, and still the protest from Detroit and its representatives continue.

During the 1940s and 1950s American banking and American business enjoyed a field day in Japan. American firms invested in hundreds of Japanese firms. When the balance of trade showed that Japan was earning enormous profits, much of those profits were coming back to America either as interest or return on venture capital. It was not until the late 1970s that the complaints in the U.S. began as the *zaikai* achieved a position where they could return the favor, and with the American recession of 1979–82, gain a strong position of investment in the United States.

From the point of view of the *zaikai*, U.S. withdrawal from Southeast Asia represented a warning that the Americans were not always to be trusted. Japan could not, of course, control American governmental policies. The ending of the Korean War had not been a shock; that war wound down, and war industries in the United States and Japan had some time to accommodate themselves to it. But the relatively sudden pullout of the Americans from Southeast Asia created a shock whose waves by the middle of the 1980s had not completely subsided. And some of those waves affected the *zaikai* and their thinking about the future. From the standpoint of the cartels the best of all possible worlds is one in which Japan completely dominates her own environment and is in no way economically subject to the political vagaries of another country, including, and perhaps especially, the United States.

In 1984 the *zaikai* were enjoying the transition from military dependence on the United States to a partnership, though the U.S. made it clear that Japan's role was to be that of junior partner. Still, in the mid-1980s there could have been no objection to that role in Japan, since she was not militarily able to fend for herself after forty years of protection by America. But what will happen when Japan's military expands? It is already the third naval power in the world, and the agreement to protect the sea lanes for a thousand miles around Japan necessitates the enormous strengthening of its air arm.

In the 1990s Japan will surely have to make some hard decisions about its future. And the *zaikai*, still dependent on American weaponry and American licenses to manufacture weaponry in Japan, is just as surely doing in the military field what it has done so thoroughly in other fields—conducting a pervasive program of research and development kept entirely secret.

In the 1990s the *zaikai* will be ready for a substantial change of direction, and the *zaikai* relationship to Japan's political arena will continue very much as in the 1930s. The industrialists and the conservative wing of Japanese political life, as exemplified by the Liberal Democratic party, will be hand in hand. Given the realities of Japanese politics, no one should expect that relationship to change.

14

Through the Looking Glass: The U.S., Japan and the Pacific

During the last years of the nineteenth century the United States pursued a policy of, in effect, imperialism, although few have been willing to say so. Americans like to think of themselves as a historically selfless, generous people with no territorial ambitions. But some facts collide with the perception. Samoa, Guam, Puerto Rico and the Hawaiian Islands speak for themselves. To be sure American policy also had moments of genuine enlightment, as in the refusal of the U.S. to participate in the dismemberment of the Chinese empire and the ultimate decision in the 1920s (after a long rebellion by the Filipinos) that the Philippines should be free in the 1940s.

At the end of the Pacific War the United States again acquired new colonies, justified by the necessities of maintaining the peace and of self-defense. The old Japanese Pacific mandate was taken over and more, including the Ryukyus. When they proved not to

175

be the assets the military had believed they would be, Okinawa and the rest of the Ryukyus went back to Japan. Truk and Saipan and other areas of the south and central Pacific secured their basic independence though with a defense commitment and other special arrangements with the United States.

At the end of the Pacific War the United States also assumed the responsibility of policing the Pacific. Having been entangled by historical commitments to the Nationalist regime of China, the United States had backed the wrong horse in the Chinese revolution, and even when almost all was lost had refused to accept the de facto change in power there, thereby pitting herself against the Beijing government. The year 1949 was a bad one for U.S. foreign policy in Asia; the inability to come to grips with Korean unification led to a feeling of frustration and virtual abandonment of South Korea. The North Koreans sensed the power vacuum and moved to attack. Entrapped by the uncomfortable alliance with Chiang Kai-shek, the U.S. oversimplified the geopolitics of Asia and stumbled in Korea until the Chinese perceived that General MacArthur offered a major threat to their borders and sent half a million troops down into Korea. Under the circumstances the American extrication from Korea with a return to the status quo ante 1950 was a considerable accomplishment, requiring an enormous staying power in the face of a recalcitrant General MacArthur and impatient public opinion.

At the end of the Korean War the Japanese felt that the United States had lived up to its commitment to South Korea, and so it felt reasonably comfortable depending on the American defense umbrella to prevent major war. During the 1960s the U.S. defense umbrella was untested and so remained a positive factor in Japanese-American relations. As noted, the question of Americans bringing atomic weapons into Japan on American warships was neatly sidestepped by both governments—the Japanese government never asked. When some organization did ask, the U.S. replied: "The U.S. navy does not confirm or deny the presence of nuclear weapons on ships," and the Japanese government allowed that answer to suffice, even through the visit of the U.S. atomic carrier *Carl Vinson* in December of 1984.

As the American involvement in Vietnam deepened in the 1960s the Japanese prospered greatly. The general prosperity of the American bloc during the war enabled the Japanese, with American financial backing, to invest enormous amounts of money in capital improvements to industry. The Japanese government assisted with tax breaks on machinery and capital accumulation and special rules for the export industry that were even more favorable. All these changes were made in the interest of the *zaibatsu*. But the oil crunch of 1973 brought on by the jump in prices by OPEC nations created serious problems in the Japanese economy, and the difficulty grew with the pullout of American forces from Vietnam in 1975, creating not only a power vacuum but an economic vacuum as well.

The Japanese now felt their main line of defense, the American military, and the American policy behind it, was a sometime thing. A president, Lyndon Johnson, gave up a race for reelection, so unpopular had the Vietnam experience become. Vice-President Hurbert Humphrey, refused to repudiate his president and so lost the election to Nixon. Viewing the U.S. public's growing distaste for war, feeling that the U.S. government did not always live up to its promises, that the long-range promises of one administration were not necessarily going to be kept by the next, the Japanese began to view their future and the alliance with the U.S. somewhat differently.

In the spring of 1972 Admiral Kenichi Kitamura, commander of the Japanese SDF naval forces, suggested publicly that Japan should have its own nuclear submarines and nuclear aircraft carriers. Since that time, privately, a number of Japanese military people have indicated the need for a Japanese nuclear *capability*. Distrust of a U.S. ability or willingness to perform in time of need was surely at least a contributor to such a tilt.

By 1984 there was little question about Japan's ability to perform in the nuclear field. She was the fourth nation to launch a space satellite; her technology in weapons systems was advanced, although what it had put on line was minimal. Americans knew how fine her technology was, and one of the points of argument in the mid-1980s was the American demand that Japan share her advanced technology with the U.S., something the *zaikai* has not been eager to do, feeling it would reduce its competitive position with foreign firms. Mitsubishi, for example, designed and built a new aircraft brought out in 1984, which was immediately accepted by the American civil aviation authorities, something that has not often happened even with American products. It was a sign of the skill the Japanese aviation industry had not lost with the destruction of the Zero, the Shiden fighter and other effective aircraft of World War II. Sometime after the war the Japanese found disassembled aircraft in an old factory. They were long-range bombers with greater capability than the B-29. These were perfected, though never put into production. As noted, by 1970 Japan was producing most of her own war matériel, largely under license from American firms, but how much longer would Japan actually need the licenses?

As for the Japanese Self-Defense Forces, the relatively small size was deceptive. The forces had to be regarded as a cadre, capable of rapid expansion in time of need. And if the Japanese government was successful in bringing about the proarmament consensus, and the Japanese public began to honor the military as they had in the 1930s, it was and is conceivable that Japan could be militarily independent within four or five years. After all, by 1984 Japanese naval and air strength in the Pacific was surpassed only by that of the Soviet Union and of the United States.

Despite visits of state and friendly talk between Japan and the South Korean government in the summer of 1984, there persisted a basic Korean distrust of Japan and a belief that if Japanese militarism were to revive, Korea would be the logical first victim of it. Part of this feeling was historic; Japan and Korea were quarreling through the pages of history: the second attempt by Kublai Khan to invade Japan was launched from Korean ports as well as Chinese. The Japanese took over Korea early in the twentieth century, and the Koreans remember that bitterly enough. And yet, when former president Park Chung Hee and Former Japanese Prime Minister Nobosuke Kishi were talking one day in Seoul late in the 1960s Kishi told Park that the United States did not have the staying power to remain in Southeast Asia and that it would eventually withdraw from South Korea too. Park told Kishi he agreed. "Japan is the only nation that can be trusted in Asia," he said. That remark represented a strong segment of Japanese and other Asian society in the last quarter of the twentieth century. Meanwhile, despite the ups and downs of international finance, the Japanese economy continued to grow and Japan continued to find new markets. In the fall of 1984 Kim Il Sung's North Korean People's Republic changed its basic laws to permit joint ventures with foreign capital. Waiting in the wings for this move, which had been anticipated—if not masterminded—by the Japanese *zai-kai*, were the old trading firms that knew Korea so well from the past.

The Japanese were also moving on the heels of the Sino-Japanese high-government exchanges. The Chinese had let it be known that they were looking with a friendly eye to introduction of foreign capital. Suddenly Japanese entrepreneurs appeared with plans under their arms. One was for a major center in Beijing to include a twenty-three-story hotel, a six-story office block for foreign business and a fourteen-story apartment block for foreign businessmen. It would be a joint venture with the Chinese. Another firm, in league with Tokyo's Hotel Okura entrepreneurs, planned to build a thirty-story hotel in Shanghai, using Japanese capital entirely. And a Kyushu supermarket chain planned to enter the Chinese market in Guilin.

The Japanese were showing once more that their flexibility and their government's support of trade with all comers was going to keep them at the top of the economic heap. In the fall of 1984, despite mutual concerns about defense and aggression, the Japanese government sent several representatives of the Diet to Moscow to try to better relations. In every way the Japanese were showing a fluidity unmatched elsewhere in the West.

An economic high-water mark was hit in the summer of 1984 when Dai Ichi Bank announced that its assets had risen to $110 billion, moving the bank from eighth in the world in total assets to the top. Dai Ichi Bank became the largest bank in the world. Citibank of New York was second, Bank of America was third, Fuji Bank was fourth, Sumitomo Bank was fifth, the Banque Nationale de Paris was sixth, Mitsubishi Bank was seventh, Barclay's Bank of London was eighth, Sanwa Bank was ninth and Credite Agricole Mutuel of Paris was tenth.

In Japan the central power structures of five of the six big cartels were numbered among the top ten banks of the world. It can reasonably be said that Tokyo in 1985 had become the financial capital of the world, a situation that had apparently not penetrated the consciousness of the United States and Western Europe.

Clearly this predominance of Japanese capital meant that Japan had an enormous position to protect, and the *zaikai* cartels were certainly not about to let it go down the drain through inattention to national defense. How that defense developed had become the major problem of the Japanese government; the government showed its recognition of the problem, and the building of the defense consensus was thereafter well underway.

In his spring trip of 1984 when Japanese Socialist leader Masashi Ishibashi traveled to the U.S. and met with various officials including Secretary of Defense Caspar Weinberger, he made the usual Socialist call for "an unarmed, neutral Japan" as a bulwark of Pacific peace. Weinberger, of course, demurred, and repeated the American view of the need for strong Japanese defenses for mutual effort, particularly at the moment around the sea lanes one thousand miles from Japan. But when Ishibashi returned home from the United States, that Japanese Socialist party policy began to change. The Socialists had seen the rapid development of the defense consensus and had realized that if they were to remain in the mainstream of Japanese life they were going to have to make some concessions to changing public opinion. Socialist objection to Japanese rearmament was toned down.

• • •

As mentioned, Japanese faith in the depth of the American commitment to defense of the Pacific was not very deep. Given the behavior of the United States in the Pacific between 1975 and 1980, Japan's feeling was perhaps not surprising. Following the U.S. withdrawal from Saigon the U.S. was viewed as behaving as though it wished it were back in the 1930s, living in a cocoon of isolationism. Such a tendency was reversed in 1981 when the Reagan administration came to power, but in the campaigns of 1984 the Democratic candidate called for a nuclear freeze and cuts in the U.S. defense budget, none of which were reassuring to Japan.

In 1983 from Tokyo, U.S. Ambassador Mike Mansfield made some important statements that merited more serious attention than they apparently got in Washington. America's two-way trade with East Asia, the ambassador noted, consistently exceeded that of Western Europe. He predicted the continued swing of American trade to the Pacific away from the Atlantic: "America's future lies with this region and the key to the development of the huge Pacific Basin area is the Japan-U.S. relationship," said Mansfield, "the most important bilateral relationship in the world, bar none."

Ambassador Mansfield was encouraged that the Reagan administration seemed to understand that importance. The 1984 annual war games indicated a growing sense of the interdependence of the Pacific Basin states. In 1979 Prime Minister Masayoshi Ohira tried to get the Americans to accept inclusion of Australia in the summit group of the Pacific. He failed. The U.S. had come a long way since then, but not far enough to gain the confidence of Asians needed to put together a sturdy Pacific Commonwealth, which had to be one of the ways of assuring that Japanese militarism did not get out of control.

Ambassador Mansfield's service in Tokyo began in the 1970s. One story he liked to tell in Japan said a great deal about Japanese-American relations:

A Japanese businessman came to Mansfield shortly after he had arrived to discuss a problem involving the U.S. steel industry, which was objecting strenuously to Japanese competition.

"You are our uncle," said the Japanese gentleman. "We come to you for advice and counsel."

"I am not your uncle," said the ambassador. "Nor are we Americans your uncle. We are brothers. The Japanese and Americans operate on an equal basis and we should talk to each other as equals because that's what we are. The Japanese should be less polite, less modest and stand up for what they think is right."

In 1985 the Japanese were doing that, and not all Americans shared Ambassador Mansfield's gratification with the result. But the ambassador's view of Japan closely coincides with that of Prime Minister Nakasone and the other leaders of the Liberal Democratic party: Japan has become not just a great economic power but has to be a great power as well.

"The Japanese have not been too anxious to accept that concept, to accept reality. But that's the way things are," said the ambassador.

The 1983 visit of President Reagan to Tokyo did a good deal to strengthen Japan's regard for the United States. It did not solve the trade problems but it did help the Japanese government in its drive for a defense consensus. Still, one of the remaining problems of the defense program was what the Americans would expect in the future. Testifying before Congress in 1984, Admiral Robert L. J. Long, former commander-in-chief, Pacific, said that Japan should be urged to block the vital international straits (Soya, Shimonoseki, Korea, Malacca, Formosa) rather than defend the shipping lanes. That testimony was contrary to the prevailing U.S defense wisdom, which seemed to be leaning toward limitless Japanese defense expansion, not excluding nuclear capability.

Admiral Long also said in front of Congress that a major buildup of Japanese military force could destabilize East Asia. The U.S., he felt, ought to relax the pressure. But there were dangers: that Japan might feel threatened that the U.S. would do something especially provocative, or, equally disastrous, the total withdrawal of U.S. forces from east Asia, as was once considered by Washington under the Carter administration. The latter could be the final straw to force Japan into either a major rearmament program, or a neutral stance toward the USSR.

The fact was that in 1984 not only Japan but China, Taiwan and the ASEAN countries of Thailand, the Philippines, Malaysia, Singapore, Indonesia and Brunei all were concerned about American willingness to pursue its current policies over the long haul. During the years since 1945 they had seen many changes in the American view and the Americans' actions, ranging from belligerence to the backlash of isolationism, from a statesmanlike rebuilding policy (the Marshall Plan) to hysterical anticommunism that made no differentiation between East and West or national and international aims. They had seen the rise of bipartisan foreign policy in the 1940s and its demise before the end of the decade. They had seen the U.S. adhere to the Nationalist government long after it ceased to represent China, to ignore the Beijing government long after it had consolidated its power, and to move quixotically vis-à-vis China and Vietnam. America-watchers could understand that the United States government was in the final analysis responsive to public opinion, but that was not particularly encouraging to peoples whose futures would depend on American actions if they put themselves in American hands.

Japan's responses to these questions had been slow and tentative:

In 1973, studying the question of Japanese rearmament, John K. Emmerson and William A. Humphreys had suggested that Japan would rearm, but never in a nuclear fashion and never offensively.

In a monograph on the Japanese defense debate in 1980 Tetsuya Kataoka of Saitama University suggested that the extent of Japanese rearmament would depend on outside influences—specifically the perception of threat to Japan.

By 1982 John H. Holdridge, assistant secretary of state from East Asian and Pacific affairs, suggested that the threat had been perceived in the Soviet military buildup in East Asia, the militarization of the northern islands that are still claimed by Japan, the Soviet assertion of raw power in Afghanistan and the military pressure against Poland.

In 1982 the United States representatives spoke of a "productive partnership" between the U.S. and Japan that was to reach an equilibrium, the Americans and the Japanese pursuing common interests around the globe. Mr. Holdridge told a congressional committee that they could be sure Japan would not seek a nuclear or offensive conventional military capability.

"Perhaps that most important bond of all between our two countries," he said, "is that which we sometimes take for granted: our dedication to essentially the same democratic form of government, honoring the same basic freedoms and individual rights."

In 1983 came the Soviet destruction in midair of a South Korean airliner, killing 269 people, to add to the pressures building in Japan for increased rearmament. By the summer of 1984 the U.S. government expressed itself as pleased with the "significant progress" made by Japan in meeting the American demands for defense and security cooperation. "The environmental and social problems connected with the American military presence in Japan have largely abated," said Paul D. Wolfowitz, then assistant secretary of state for East Asian and Pacific affairs. "Over the past two years," Wolfowitz went on, "there has been a significant change in Japanese attitudes toward its own self-defense... the existence of the Japanese Self-Defense Forces is now accepted by an overwhelming majority of the Japanese people. But the most important change over the past two years is what I perceive as a new understanding in Japan of the real reasons why an enhanced defense effort is necessary. For many years in our security relationship Japanese governments very often took the steps that they did in the defense arena and justified them to their people by saying that they were necessary for the sake of the U.S.-Japan relationship. Increasingly in Japan, government leaders, politicians and opinion makers have come to realize that this is something that must be done, not simply to "satisfy the Americans," but because it is in Japan's own national interest. There, therefore, has been a qualitative difference in the way the Japanese government and people look at defense issues."

Even before the Japanese government decision to seek the defense consensus, the government began stepping up its defense expenditures. From 1981 to 1985 the average increase in Japanese defense spending was 5 percent per year as compared to the NATO allies' increase of 2 percent per year. In 1984 the Diet passed a no-increase budget, but defense expenditures were up over 6 percent.

Still, the Americans pressed for more. "... the level of spending," said Mr. Wolfowitz, "will not be sufficient to allow it to implement the Mid-Term Defense Plan, or within this decade, the defense roles and missions that it has set out for itself."

So more and more was to be demanded by America. But if the Japanese produced more and more, was it reasonable to assume they would continue to accept the role of junior partner?

Within the United States in the 1980s there were calls for cuts in defense, especially cuts in the rate of increase in expenditures. Such cuts would require, presumably, other countries to undertake greater shares of the common defense. In the 1984 hearings before the Subcommittee on Asian and Pacific Affairs of the U.S. House of Representatives, subcommittee Chairman Stephen Solarz, New York Democrat, several times asked witnesses how Japan could be induced to rearm faster to ease the American burden.

That was in May, 1984. An indication of the rapidity with which Prime Minister Nakasone was moving the government effort toward the defense consensus was to be found in other testimony that month. Professor Gerald L. Curtis of Columbia University was one of America's prime Japan-watchers. In May, 1984, he testified before the same congressional subcommittee to say: "The Japanese do not feel a threat, [and] until the Japanese perception is similar to ours they are not going to have a military policy similar to ours." Admiral Long had been even less convinced that Japan was ready for major rearmament: "I am not convinced that the political will is there," he said.

It was apparent that the admiral and the professor needed a new visit to Tokyo. It was no longer a question of the political will of the government and its adherents. The search for consensus was on, and it would be only a matter of time before the government had the public backing it for extensive movement in rearmament.

As of 1985 there could be no question about the will of the Japanese government to impress on its people the need for increased defense. But within that framework the idea of contributing to a joint American-Japanese defense pattern was not necessarily the only road considered. As Mr. Wolfowitz said, in the past Japanese governments had frequently justified defense policies by saying they were taken to pacify the Americans. That attitude goes back to 1946 when the Japanese cabinet sacrificed (but only on paper) Japan's entire defense establishment in exchange for the life of the emperor. The pacifist constitution was, in fact, the invention of the Japanese politicians to please the conquerors, and many of them foresaw that it could never last.

In 1984 there were elements in Japan calling for the nation to take a political position commensurate with its economic position. The old concept of defense alone had already been discarded by the leaders of the Self-Defense Forces, who were talking of the need to have an offensive capability as well. By the end of the year the government was discussing the possibility of sending Japanese forces abroad for United Nations peacekeeping operations, as another step in its growing independence. The American military had never suggested this action; it was a suggestion first made by the U.S.-Japan Advisory Commission, some UN members having suggested that Japan ought to take a greater role in world affairs.

Such an increase in military activity seemed a natural and unavoidable consequence of Japan's growing economic power. But it brought its worrisome concomitants, most serious of which was a concern over the point at which a newly legitimized and respectable defense establishment would be willing to stop.

In the search for the defense consensus, Prime Minister Nakasone took the next step in the fall of 1984. In the summer he had opened the matter of education; a few weeks later he began talking about the need for "moral education," as an essential part of educational reform in Japan.

The Ministry of Education was already putting emphasis on so-called moral education, and so were some 90 percent of Japanese schools. A poll by the Japan Public Opinion Research Association showed that 75 percent of people surveyed wanted more moral education. And what did that mean? To most educators it meant teaching the "indomitable spirit." And what was "the indomitable spirit"? To many it was the spirit of the old Japan, the uniform spiritual education in school before and during the war. Comparison of several sets of statements is worth considering:

> We seek to create in Japan an interdependent unity based on a moral concept of society, and internationally a mutually helpful common welfare for mankind growing out of a moral world view . . .
>
> —Foreign Minister Yosuke
> Matsuoka, 1938

> It is an urgent matter for Japan to realize the establishment of a structure of national unanimity in politics, economy, culture, education and all other realms of national life.
>
> —Japanese Ministry of
> Education, 1941

> After the defeat in World War II, Confucian and Buddhist morality made way for individualism. As it turned out, violence and selfishness prevailed. It is high time that we reviewed Japan's present spiritual civilization in an attempt to give a new dimension to school education.
>
> —Prime Minister Yasuhiro
> Nakasone, 1984

The U.S. seemed to be behind the times. The "new spirit" in Japan existed and was moving rapidly toward a new Japanese view of the world and the Japanese place in it. Or was it new? Was it instead the revival of a very old Japanese concept?

By 1985 Japan had achieved a new national pride in economic accomplishment and was being pressed to match that with a new military presence. By the end of 1984 the dreams of the Americans and the Japanese defense establishment were well on their way to fruition.

The real problem would be in the future, when brakes would be needed if Japan was not once again to go her own lonely way in the Pacific.

28 | Bazookas, submachine guns, and automatic rifles are all part of the Japanese modern arsenal.

29 | Motorcycle units are a regular part of the Japanese Defense Force.

30

31

32

30 | American training. Japanese Self–Defense Force troops learn the use of the most modern U.S. equipment.

31 | Japanese Maritime Defense Force unit at sea. In 1984 the Japanese destroyer force operated as a unit with the U.S. Pacific Fleet for the first time.

32 | American and Japanese officers getting a briefing on Hokkaido maneuvers.

33 | American and Japanese infantrymen on maneuvers.

34 | Winter maneuvers include siting and operating field artillery under frigid conditions.

35 | The Long Stairway. Behind that door at the top rest mementos of Lord Nelson, John Paul Jones and Admiral Togo. The museum is dedicated to the portrayal of great moments in Japanese naval history, including the days of the kamikaze suicide pilots of World War II.

15

Are the Words of the Past the Words of the Future?

*We must progress to a new kind of world control.
In accordance with this, we must prepare a new
national educational policy.*

> —"A Plan for Educational
> Mobilization,"
> Takeya Fushimi, 1940

*My feeling is that the cultures of colored races will
be emerging conspicuously with Japan as a central
force . . . The Japanese ought to produce a new
culture which is larger in scale and different in
quality from the conventional ones, and thereby to
help unite the wisdom of peoples in both cultures for
the creation of a new breed of culture.*

> —Prime Minister Yasuhiro
> Nakasone, 1984

One day in 1984 in Tokyo U.S. Ambassador Mike Mansfield was
asked by a Japanese reporter about his understanding of Japan.
Mansfield replied in a Japanese fashion: During his six-and-a-half
years he had traveled in every Japanese prefecture. He had learned
a great deal. He still had much to learn. He had read constantly,
all sorts of articles by Americans about Japan. "They are usually
referred to as being experts on Japan. But there is no such person
because I don't think anybody, certainly a reporter, can understand
what the Japanese themselves do not understand."

189

The ambassador's remark was an assessment of the enormous difficulty in watching the movement of public policy in Japan, as in the 1984–85 national debate over Japan's defense stance. For the fact was that nothing in Japanese political life was precisely as it seemed on the surface.

In the autumn of 1984, on the eve of the Japanese Liberal Democratic party internal elections, the LDP and the left wing were tilting at the lists over the matter of defense policy. But the argument was not so waged; rather the important discussions concerned educational reform in Japan, which, on the surface, is a long way from defense matters.

Late in August, after giving many signals, the Nakasone government submitted to the Diet a list of twenty-five members of an ad hoc council on educational reform. Glaringly missing from the list were the names of any members of the Nikkyoso, the Japan Teachers Union. The union had declared a boycott of the advisory council on the ground that the panel could not strike any national consensus on educational reforms because the majority of members were businessmen, bureaucrats and Nakasone followers. But the real reason for the boycott was political and philosophical: The leftist Nikkyoso was already on record as saying that Nakasone's plans for educational reform were really plans to restore Japan to the old Imperial Way, the militarism of the 1930s and 1940s.

"The Nakasone government," said Ichiro Tanaka, president of the Japan Teachers Union, "is trying to obstruct postwar democratic education based on the constitution and the Basic Education Law." He blamed the *zaikai* as much as the government; indeed, he charged that the Nakasone government's efforts came in response to demands from the industrialists. In the spring Nikkyoso had declared war on the concept, and since then had done everything possible to scuttle the council plan. It would rally all its force, said Tanaka, to prevent the plan from getting off the ground. The teacher's union had done just that, and it had lost.

Predictably, the Diet split on the issue. The Socialists and the Communists criticized Nakasone for trying to tighten state control of education. Komeito, the party of the Nichiren Buddhist Soka

Gakkai that was second in importance in Japan, and the Democratic Socialist party, which was more akin to the LDP than the Socialists, supported the Nakasone position. So the debate was on.

The reality was not easily understood by foreigners. What was apparent, however, was that except for the far left, the advisory council did represent a wide range of Japanese thinking. The one great void was lack of representation of the public high school teachers, who had enormous prestige in the communities.

Otherwise, here is a basic list of the participants:

Name	Representing
Isao Nakauchi	Business (Daiei supermarkets)
Harumi Kimura	College educator
Naohiro Dogakinai	Politics (ex-governor of Hokkaido)
Yoshiji Miyata	Iron and steelworkers
Michio Okamoto	Educator (ex-president Kyoto University)
Tadao Ishikawa	Educator (rector, Keio University)
Sohei Nakayama	Banker
Naohiro Amaya	Bureaucrat (Ministry of Trade)
Takemochi Ishii	Engineering professor
Hidenobu Kanasugi	Labor leader
Ryuzo Sejima	Army ex-staff officer, Imperial Army
Atsuo Tobari	Educator (high school)
Kazuhisa Arita	Educator (adult)
Toshitsugu Saito	Junior Chamber of Commerce
Shunichiro Okano	Japan Olympic Committee
Noboru Kabayashi	Medical professor
Kenichi Koyama	Law professor
Soichi Iihima	College administrator
Tadashi Minakami	School administration
Akiyo Tamaru	Primary school teacher
Sei Saito	Ministry of Education
Ryozo Sunobe	Foreign Ministry
Akayo Sono	Christian novelist

Kenzo Uchida   Journalist
Takashi Hosomi   International philanthropy
                           (president of the Overseas
                           Economic Cooperation Fund)

The only surprise in the list was the inclusion of a former Imperial Army officer. Even ten years earlier it would have been impossible. His area of interest was "to develop a man of physical strength, virtue and knowledge."

Here, in this commission, lay one of the keys to Japan's future. After appointing the council, Prime Minister Nakasone said he wanted it to study changes in the educational system that would in the future allow Japan to fit better into the world community as "internationally minded individuals, their spiritual and physical education having adequately prepared them to cope" with the new science, technology and information society. And "*The relevance of Japanese cultural, spiritual and traditional values should be studied by the council in relation to postwar educational reform.*" (Italics, author's.)

The problem of Japan, as seen by the conservative government, was forty years of spiritual drift. Soka Gakkai, of course, could not have agreed more; its ultimate goal was to turn Japan totally to Nichiren Buddhism. One major concern at the end of 1983 was the rise in juvenile delinquency in a country where forty years earlier the concept had been unthinkable. The same story could be told, of course, in any Western country, but Japan, in spite of her adaptation since the 1940s, was not a Western country and there were many in the society who objected ever more strenuously to Western ways as injurious to the Japanese way of life. In the mid-1980s, despite superficial appearances such as the decline in wearing of the kimono, 70 percent of Japanese nuclear families were, like the families of the 1940s, built around the husband, and the statistics were the same for all age groups. Beneath the tinsel and hoopla of the television world dwelled a Japan that was very unlike the West.

Late in the summer of 1984 the *Japan Times* made a study of

Nakasone's speeches and writings over the years to try to anticipate the direction in which his leadership would take the nation.
Since the end of the Pacific War, from which he had emerged as
one of the naval officers dishonored by the American victors,
Nakasone had concerned himself with the future of a dislocated
Japanese society. One of his early actions was to form an organization dedicated to restoration of nationalism, Seiunjuku. Here
are some of the Nakasone concepts:

*The spirit of Seiunjuku . . . the soul of cosmopolitan Japanese and rugged
individualism . . . patriotism for making Japan an independent nation.*

*The passion deriving from this spirit appeals for the democratic creation of the
Constitution, promotion of the retreat of the Occupation Forces, control of nuclear
and conventional arms by an international body, a Japan for workers with labor
and science as axes, a society with many middle-class people, and the construction
of a fraternity nation that extends a loving hand to people with grief and sufferings.*

Nakasone wanted Japan to return to basics in everything, from
swimming to patterns of behavior.

*We can still say that postwar Japan still does not have any important system
of ideas that functions as a central pillar for rebuilding our nation. In the past,
ideas such as farmer democracy and militarism made the Japanese people pas-
sionately chauvinistic. The fact shows that those ideas were attractive and contained some appealing truth. Today we uphold democracy and pacifism. But why
don't we have the kind of fervor we once had for militarism or farmer democracy?*

These are excerpts from a speech to students made by Nakasone
when he was rector of Takushoku University. Since that time
Nakasone had ceased to uphold pacifism. As for democracy, some,
including the socialists, claimed that Japanese democracy was no
more than skin deep, and given the direction proposed by Nakasone, would be shucked off in the process of rebuilding Japan as
a world power.

Nakasone took a more transcendental view of the Japanese total
problem:

The best way for the Japanese race to follow is to make Japan one of the world's leading cultural countries for the cause of attaining fusion between Oriental and Occidental cultures. This may sound like big talk to you. But according to my intuition, Occidental culture is most likely to converge into the American culture in a matter of half to one century. When we go to Europe we feel the eclipse of the European races. Then, how about the races of colored people? My feeling is that the cultures of colored races will be emerging conspicuously with Japan as a central force. As put by Professor Toynbee there is a high possibility that the realization of "challenge and response" would be established between the two rising cultures over the Pacific.

Taking this to heart we must strive to build this country into the one representing Oriental culture or culture of colored people and to make the Japanese race capable of materializing cultural fusion and interchange in peace.

I firmly believe that to propagate a certain culture with recourse to wars or arms is an outmoded manner. The Japanese ought to produce a new culture which is large in scale and different in quality from the conventional ones and thereby help unite the wisdom of peoples in both cultures for the creation of a new breed of culture.

The key to Nakasone's dream, of course, is the word "how." The Japanese of the Imperial Way also had such a dream:

Cease holding the policies and principles of the past, laying aside the spirit of dependence, improve our internal governmental affairs, make our country secure by military preparation, and then wait for the time of the confusion of Europe, which must come eventually sooner or later; and although we have no immediate concern with it ourselves we must feel it, for such an event will agitate the nations of the Orient as well, and then, although our country is not mixed up in the matter so far as Europe is concerned, we may then become the chief nation of the Orient.

—Viscount Tani, 1887

The viscount was a visionary, seeing the disruption of the Western colonial powers and the emergence of Japan as Asia's leader. In the 1980s one could almost substitute America for Europe and repeat the lines.

At the time of the Meiji restoration Japan perfected her national structure to defy foreign aggression, and since then the country has been increasing in national strength and has succeeded in realizing the building up of a rich national economy and a strong military power.

> —"The Way of Subjects," Japanese Ministry of Education, July, 1941.

This could be said to be the renewed Japanese goal of the 1980s.

There will be no country that can compete with Japan when the Japanese become true Japanese again, and united. There are some who are pessimistic because Japan is now short of materials. Materials are important, of course, but there is something more important, the spiritual forces.

> —Toyama Mitsui, leader of the Black Dragon Society, in *Asahi Shimbun*, August 30, 1941

This leader of the sometimes misunderstood Black Dragon Society was deeply concerned with the national spirit. The society was active in the 1920s, and some of its activities were indeed bizarre, some dangerous, all done in the interest of patriotism, the force Prime Minister Nakasone's government was setting back into play in 1984.

The Manchuria incident and the China affair are nothing but manifestations of Japan's attempt to forestall the destruction of civilization. The Manchuria incident should be termed the start of construction, not destruction, of world peace. The Co-Prosperity Sphere in the Far East is based on the spirit of Hakko Ichiu, of the Eight Corners of the Universe under One Roof. It is not that America's leaders don't understand this, but that they don't try to understand it.

> —Yosuke Matsuoka, Japanese foreign minister, in speech to Diet, January 17, 1941

Yosuke Matsuoka, however, certainly understood his America and his English language. During the crisis over Manchuria in the

League of Nations, Matsuoka appeared as a special ambassador in Geneva and made a speech in colloquial English, so moving an address that it half-convinced some delegates that Japan was *not* undertaking the aggression that the world really knew she was doing in Manchuria.

Matsuoka knew his Americans, too. He had gone to the United States as a small boy and worked his way through the University of Oregon. He knew Americans and their prejudices against colored peoples, and he had a fine-honed hatred for the United States. Matsuoka is long gone, but Japanese resentment against Western treatment of the past is no more forgotten than the occupation.

Nippon's guiding principle of defense is non-aggression and non-menace. . . . The Greater East Asia autarchic sphere which Nippon endeavors to consolidate involves no territorial aggrandizement.
—Masami Shimoda, Japanese
Nationalist, 1941

In 1941 the people of Japan believed those words. The Manchuria incident was to them no more than protection of the enormous Japanese investment the Chinese had earlier permitted. The China affair was to Japan's public the protection of Japanese trading interests in China against a selfish Nationalist Chinese government.

Words, words, words! They can be used, as they were by the Japanese militarists of the 1930s, to mean whatever one wants them to mean.

Japan is proceeding with the task of building up a lasting peace in East Asia, in accordance with the spirit of the principle which inspired the founding of the Empire. We must anticipate formidable difficulties in order to bring the task to completion. We must see that there is perfect unity within the nation and to give first attention to the perfecting of a highly developed national defense structure.
—Finance Minister Kawada, before
the Diet, January 21, 1941

Minister Kawada's statment could have come from the mouth of Prime Minister Nakasone himself, with his twin concerns for the national spirit and the national defense.

The problem with words, and especially Japanese words translated into foreign languages, is the matter of real meaning.

Sometimes the understanding is easy enough:

Deceit may be pardoned in proportion to the benefits it confers.
—Minister of State Yukio Azaki, 1940

Ways and means need not be regarded if the object required is attained.
                    —Viscount Miura

Sometimes it is not so simple:

The Oriental ideal of love, benevolence, and mutual help condemns war for selfish ends. Japan's armament—always a "divine sword that slays not"—is dedicated to the peace of East Asia and to the welfare of the world; it is employed only against the forces inimical to international justice and to the common interests of East Asia. Japan's advance, inspired by humanity, should not be confused with aggression for gain at the expense of other nations.
                    —Tatsuo Kaiwai, Japanese
                    publicist, 1940s

Could not these words almost be attributed to Prime Minister Nakasone in his concept of the "challenge and response" of Oriental and American civilizations? The problem is, of course, what sort of challenge? What sort of response?

Japanese is indeed a fluid language, immensely alive with innuendo and gradations of meaning, and constantly changing, more than any other language in the world with the possible exception of American English. The Japanese even more easily adopt and make over into Japanese foreign words and concepts. But their own words and concepts are not always so easily understood outside Japan. And that is why when Prime Minister Nakasone speaks of developing a new spirit in Japan to build the country into one

representing Oriental culture and "make the Japanese race capable
of materializing cultural fusion and interchange in peace," one can
conjure visions of a Buddhaesque change, all accomplished in the
most pastoral manner—or of a Masamune lopping off heads.

Another of Mr. Nakasone's statements is: "The current education system places far too much emphasis on gaining knowledge
while neglecting the importance of virtue. The system almost
ignores the importance of developing a sound body." To some
Japanese his words may not sound so different from those of
Takeya Fushimi, a political educator of the militarist school in
1940:

> *The content of education from henceforth should, instead of the old principle
> of the supreme importance of knowledge, consist equally of scientific education
> and of moral and physical training. The Japanese people, who are to advance
> from control of the Asiatic continent to control of the world, must above all have
> tough bodies and firm wills.*

A basic problem in Japan in the 1980s is going to be the rebuilding of a national pride based on solid accomplishment and
an innocent (as opposed to guilty) view of the world around it.
The accomplishment was already in place—the "economic miracle" had convinced the world that the Japanese traits of diligence
and adaptability were sound examples for the rest of the world;
it had also convinced the Japanese.

The question of a new spirit was something else. Prime Minister
Nakasone and many others spoke of a role for Japan as bridge
between East and West, and as leader of the East in a peaceful
Pacific Community. Yosuke Matsuoka and the generals of the past
made statements of that sort, even at the height of Japanese conquest:

> *Japan is the foundation and the axis of the world. The world must be unified
> around Japan. Without unity there will be no peace. When the world is unified
> under one power, then there will be eternal peace.*
> —Tokyo Radio, February, 1942

That much could be attributed to the excesses of the militarists, flushed with victory. But what of this:

Peace will come when the whole world is under one government. The worlds tend toward this at present. The ultimate conclusion of the political is the conquest of the world by one imperial power. Which nation is likely to be the conqueror of the world? That nation which is strongly united in patriotism, has unquenchable imperial ambitions and willingness to make every sacrifice for the ultimate goal. The Japanese nation, in view of her glorious history and position, should brace herself to fill her destined role.

—Taiyo magazine, Tokyo, 1918

Japan's ultranationalism was not a creature only of the 1930s and 1940s. It was an essential part of the Meiji restoration, and predates even that so-called turning point:

Among the rulers of the world at present, there is none so noble and illustrious as to command universal vassalage, or who can make his virtue felt throughout the length and breadth of the whole world. To have such a ruler over the whole world is doubtless in conformity with the will of Heaven. In establishing relations with foreign countries the object should always be kept in view of laying the foundation for securing hegemony over all nations. The national resources should be developed and military preparations vigorously carried out. When our power and national standing have come to be recognized we should take the lead in punishing the nations which may act contrary to the principal of international interest. We should declare our protection over harmless but powerful nations. Such a policy could be nothing but enforcement of the power and authority deputed to us by the Spirit of Heaven. Our national prestige and position thus ensured, the nations of the world will come to look up to our emperor as the Great Ruler of all the nations, and they will come to follow our policy and submit to our judgment. This ideal realized, the Ruler of Japan will have accomplished a deed commensurate with the great responsibilities he owes to Heaven and Earth.

—Lord Hatta, who negotiated the
treaty with the United States for
the opening of Japan, in a
memorial submitted to the throne,
1858

When America urges Japan to rearm, then, the Japanese records and the Japanese *kokutai* or polity of the past indicate the risk that the changes developed in the national consensus for the abandonment of pacifism in favor of a new sort of limited militarism will go much further than perhaps the politicians of the 1980s might wish.

16

Japan Rearms

On December 6, 1984, Prince Norihito, the third son of Prince Mikasa, and a nephew of the emperor of Japan, married Hisako Tottori, the daughter of a Tokyo trading-house executive. The ceremony was covered by television cameras, and so viewers all over Japan were treated to the sight of the royal couple in full modern evening regalia being greeted by Emperor Hirohito in white tie and tails. It was almost like a White House reception.

The prince works for the Japan Foundation, just as Yasuo Yamamoto (Joe Smith) works for Mitsubishi. He goes to the office in a business suit like any other "*sarariman.*" He is a graduate of Canada's Queens University, and his bride took a degree at Cambridge. After the wedding the imperial couple left for their honeymoon in the Kansai area of southern Honshu.

It was a very modern wedding; one might say that this marriage, prince to commoner, in Western style, represented the new Japan. And so it did—but not quite as it seemed on the surface. For the bride was no commoner. Her father had been a baron in the days before the Americans oversaw the outlawry of the peerage. In the eyes of the imperial family he was still a baron. And the pair were not married in white tie and tails and a wedding gown, as the television cameras indicated. That was the postnuptial reception. The actual wedding was an ancient Japanese ceremony, she in flowing kimono whose train scraped the tatami, and he in the traditional black robes, black cap and topknot of the imperial family. The prince is not just a *sarariman*; the imperial throne bestowed on the newlyweds a palace in Tokyo and an endowment of ¥53 million ($240,000). They will receive another ¥35,000,000 annually ($150,000) to keep up with the Mitsuis. Their honeymoon trip to Kansai was to pay homage at the Grand Shrine at Ise and the mausoleum of the Emperor Jimmu, legendary ancestor of the imperial family, who is, the Japanese believe, descended directly from the sun goddess. And the Japanese, being all part of one great family, are too.

So, as the cynical Frenchman said, the more things change the more they remain the same. Legally the emperor is just Citizen Hirohito. But anyone who believes that the man who lives in Tokyo's Imperial Palace—about four million square meters of land behind its magnificent moat that dominates the heart of Tokyo—is just another citizen, must also still believe in the tooth fairy. By that same token, anyone who believes there has been much change in the status of the imperial family through "democratization" should be heading for the North Pole to visit Santa Claus. That wedding in Tokyo in the late autumn of 1984 emphasized the "Japanese-ness" of modern Japan, the customs of which would be completely recognizable by Toyatomi Hideyoshi, who drove foreign influences out of Japan in the sixteenth century.

Certainly the Japan of 1985 is modern enough; skyscrapers, superhighways and 150-mile-an-hour trains attest to that. Certainly Japan is a triumph of twentieth-century capitalism. Certainly it is a constitutional monarchy; so was Emperor Meiji's government. Certainly the government of Japan is democratic, and controlled by the electorate. But Japan has always been capitalistic; there is no greater enmity than Japan's toward communism, although the Japanese make far less noise about it than do the Americans. And in economics Japan has always been upwardly mobile, even under the shoguns. As for the constitution, the political form and the status of the emperor, they have changed several times in the past, and may change in the future. What impressed this traveler most in five weeks in Japan in 1984 was the enormous vitality and energy of the Japanese, and their renewed confidence that Japan is going to inherit the earth. From middle-school girls running to be half an hour early to their school across the street from my Chiyoda-ku hotel, to *sararimen* dashing to catch the bullet train at Kyoto station, box lunch in hand; from the maid of the Japanese inn scrubbing down the sidewalk at 7 A.M. to the fishermen tonging for cockles in Matsue's Lake Shinji, the Japanese exhibited a remarkable vigor and adaptability.

Seiichi Soeda's is a case in point. Several years ago in his mid-fifties he was retired a colonel in the Air Defense Force to make room for younger men. Now he is the coordinator for media assistance at the Foreign Press Center in Tokyo. The center is a "private" institution; that is, it has no official connections and is supported by the media and other businesses. But the fact known to all officials is that the center is very close to the Japanese foreign office, and its unofficial standing as mentor to foreign newsmen has many uses. It is also another little sign of Japanese adaptability and skill in dealing with the outside world on terms that seem to be neutral but which are really very Japanese.

Seiichi Soeda is nearly sixty years old, yet he maintains a schedule that would put a long-distance commuter to shame. He rides the subway for an hour each morning from his Western-style condominium in one part of Tokyo to his office in another section. He goes to work at 9 A.M. and seldom leaves before 7 P.M. On weekends (only every other Saturday off) he and his family move down to their "country" place at Yokosuka on Tokyo Bay within sight of the American warships that nearly always ride at anchor there. This house is as Japanese as their condo is Western—tatami mat floors, sliding paper doors; only the color television set would be strange to Toyatomi Hideyoshi. And Seiichi Soeda turns that set on every Sunday morning at seven and tunes to NHK, the government television network, for his weekly session with his

Korean language instructor, Soeda having listened every night during the week at 11 P.M. to NHK's radio broadcast lessons. He will soon add Korean to his list of languages. His English is so good that he has won several awards and in 1983 was given a trip to America to refresh his connections with American journalists he had aided in the past; in 1984 he was sent to Australia to do the same and visited half a dozen cities. Unofficial Soeda might be, but you could also call him a semiofficial ambassador.

Seiichi Soeda has many of the qualities of a perpetual motion machine, but in this he is not unique. In travels to examine the stage of the Japanese Self-Defense Forces—from Tokyo Bay to the Sea of Japan to the Inland Sea—I found that the "retired" Soeda is very typical of the SDF. There is, from the civilians who control the ministry down to the sergeants and petty officers who make things run, an enormous competence and enthusiasm that seem to feed on themselves. The Japanese, pushed now to increase their military effort, can be expected to continue to do so, year after year. There is an element of the herd instinct in this that is a little frightening. It is like watching the beginning of a cattle stampede. For as the Japanese know better than anyone, they are a "flock people," and as such can be turned in a certain direction once a consensus is achieved and thereafter will follow that way until some vital change in direction is forced on them by events.

That is the danger inherent in Japan's military buildup.

The Defense Agency is now in transition to become a Ministry of Defense. The head of the agency is still referred to as director by the media, but within the agency he is called minister, for he is a full-fledged minister of state within the cabinet. He is a civilian as the law demands. Civilian control operates just as it does in the United States: The heads of the uniformed services make their plans and budgets, then clear them through a committee of civilian bureaucrats. The civilian minister then approves the budget, after which it goes to the Ministry of Finance and then to the cabinet and the prime minister and finally to the full Diet. At the end of 1984 the Agency had been called "Japan Self-Defense Agency."

Quietly, at the end of 1984, it became "Japan Defense Agency." It is a short way to an official Ministry of Defense.

There is a difference with the past. In Japan, before what the Japanese call Dai Too A Senso (the Great East Asia War) and Westerners call the Pacific War, the military had direct access to the fount of power—the throne—outside the approach through the cabinet. This is no longer true. In the old days the imperial nature of Japan was widely advertised by the annual photograph of the emperor in full military regalia riding his white horse. In 1985 if Hirohito still owns a white horse nobody outside the palace entourage knows about it. Hirohito is no longer head of the armed forces. It is the prime minister who reviews the troops in 1985, and wearing his civilian suit although he is a retired naval officer. Nor is there any provision as in the 1930s that the cabinet officer in charge of the armed forces be an active service officer. To the contrary, he cannot be, under the law (which is further than the U.S. law goes—General of the Army George C. Marshall was secretary of defense in the 1950s). Legally, as noted, the Japanese military under the constitution of 1946 no longer exists in spite of what one sees. That anomaly inclines an observer to caution. And there is need for caution when observing Japan, for it is easy to attribute the rise of the old militarism in Japan to the generals and admirals alone and to absolve the politicians of blame. They are the first to take that position, particularly the politicians of the Liberal Democratic party, the ruling faction in Japan. As one opposition political leader said to me: "You must not forget that for ninety-three years Japan has been ruled by the same conservative political faction." Call it the LDP or the Seiyukai, or the Kenseikai (parties of prewar Japan), they were all conservative in nature. The system of elections in Japan, the manner in which election districts are selected, the manner of representation and the gerrymandering of districts have kept the conservatives in power almost uninterruptedly—except for the few weeks of socialist experiment in the early days of the U.S. occupation—since the Meiji days.

Akira Kurayanogi, the man who made that statement, is director of international affairs for the Komeito party, which means if the party came to power he would be foreign minister. His statement indicates that the politicians, indeed, had a major responsibility for what happened in Japan in the 1930s, and the establishment of the military oligarchy of the 1940s.

Komeito, the "clean government party," asserts that in power it would control the military, uphold the constitution and protect Japan's fragile democracy. But would it really make any difference? Nearly everyone—the socialists reluctantly included—accepts the U.S.-Japan defense alliance as essential to the future welfare of Japan.

Komeito complains that the United States and Japanese governments are in "repeated violation" of the law's "three nonnuclear principles: no possession, no manufacture and no introductions of nuclear weapons [into Japan]." The U.S. repeatedly brings warships to Japan that carry nuclear Tomahawk missiles, and everybody knows it. The most recent example was the visit in 1984 of the nuclear carrier *Carl Vinson* to Yokosuka naval base. She came on December 7, the anniversary of the Pearl Harbor attack. Protestors came out to meet her and a few were arrested. Media men assembled on the quay and asked sailors if the ship was carrying nuclear weapons. "No comment," said the American sailors, and everybody smiled.

For Komeito, the media men and the protestors all knew that Tomahawk nuclear missiles and nuclear aircraft weapons are an integral part of the American defense system. If the letter of the Japanese law were observed, American warships would simply have to stop sailing in Japanese waters. As columnist Masaru Ogawa of the *Japan Times* puts it, "What would be even worse would be a U.S. decision not to make port calls at Yokosuka or Sasebo." What he meant was that the U.S. would have to rescind its promise to protect Japan.

So if Komeito came to power the government would have to accept the situation of 1984 in which U.S. authorities refuse to confirm or deny what everyone knows, and the Japanese government refuses to pry, or Japan would have to scrap the U.S. alliance and plan to defend itself by itself. That alternative in 1985 is certainly not acceptable to the majority of Japanese, no matter what doubts they may have about the American staying power for the long run.

A 1984 SDF white paper on the defense of Japan makes this fact clear, as does the government's determination to increase defense spending to the limit of the 1 percent of the GNP established by custom, and to prepare to go beyond that, probably in fiscal 1986. As of 1984 Japan already ranked eighth in the world in military spending, just behind France, just ahead of Iran.

What Japan is getting for its money is obviously the most competent and highly motivated military force in Asia—perhaps in the world. On visits to the National Defense Academy and the old Japanese naval academy at Eta Jima, now serving the same purpose as the Maritime Defense Force's officer's candidate school, I was impressed by the caliber of training and by the cadets. Above one doorway at Eta Jima hangs an old piece of Japanese calligraphy that symbolizes it all: In Pursuit of Bravery and Knowledge. There is no mea culpa here for World War II or any other. Outside the museum stands a *kaiten*—suicide submarine—to show just that.

Many of the old traditions of the Imperial Navy (see Appendix 3) have been retained at Eta Jima, and some traditions of army and navy have been passed along to the new (1952) National Defense Academy, which significantly combines into one school officer training for the three services. Located on a high bluff overlooking Yokosuka naval base, it provides a life of regimentation and hard work that will last for the next five years if officer candidates succeed and end up being commissioned as naval ensigns or second lieutenants in the air force (Air Defense Force) or army (Ground Defense Force). Here is a sample of what these young men undergo—the winter schedule at Yokosuka:

6:30 Reveille
6:35 Roll call
7:00 Breakfast

   8:05 Morning colors
   8:15 Morning formation
   8:30 Classes
 12:10 Classes end
 12:25 Luncheon
  1:20 Formation
  1:35 Classes
  5:15 Evening Colors
  5:20 Recreation, bath
  6:45 Supper
  7:20 Evening roll call
  7:30 Study
10:15 Taps

Besides official physical activity, kendo (Japanese fencing), Western fencing, gymnastics, track and field, American football, European football, rugby, baseball, basketball, swimming, sailing and boxing, the students join various clubs, ranging from karate and sumo wrestling to flower arranging, and compete ardently. Classes go through Saturday noon. Cadets may then have afternoon leave on weekends, and once a month after the first year they may have an overnight pass.

The cadets are exposed to army, navy and air force training for the first three years. They then list their career choices—one, two, three. But the authorities make the decision on the basis of record, aptitude and needs of the service. A class of five hundred young men (no women) enters each April. About fifty drop out for one reason or another in the next four years, usually for health or adaptability problems. In the thirty years of the academy there have been no drug, alcohol, sex or cheating scandals like those that periodically rock the American service schools. At the end of four years the Japanese cadets are promoted to the three special postgraduate schools for training in ground forces, air forces or navy at Kurume in Kyushu, Nara and Eta Jima. On graduation day at Yokosuka they appear in their new uniforms, and the next week they report for the next school year.

The officials of the Self-Defense Forces say that the SDF has no relationship to the old imperial forces. But a visit to Eta Jima indicated how little has changed in forty years, and bespeaking the stability and continuity is the museum. A long red-carpeted stairway inside the collonaded building leads directly from the entry to a locked door on the second floor. Behind that door are kept locks of the hair of Lord Nelson, Admiral Togo and Admiral Yamamoto. The walls of the museum are lined with glass cases; inside are letters, photos, paintings and calligraphy to tell the story of great moments in Japanese naval history, such as the battles of Formosa Strait (China War) Tsushima Strait (Russo-Japanese War) and Kiaochao (World War I). World War II is not neglected. Yamamoto's bust is here, and memorabilia noting various victories and defeats. But the pièce de résistance of the Pacific War is a whole section devoted to the twenty-two hundred naval pilots who sacrificed their lives as kamikaze, or suicide, pilots in the last months of the war. Last letters, head scarves, photos and other memorabilia fill the cases. All the names are there on a plaque. Their leaders are memorialized: Vice-Admiral Takejiro Ohnishi, who devised the concept of the kamikazes, and Vice-Admiral Matome Ugaki, who commanded the last desperate kamikaze effort from Kyushu and then flew to his death after the surrender, insisting that since he had sent so many brave men to die he must join them.

The reverence with which the Japanese naval officers regard the museum and their unbroken tradition was apparent in our museum guide, Lieutenant Commander Shigeo Hayashi, a man of the "new navy," a graduate of the National Defense Academy and of Eta Jima. As we entered the museum he took off his uniform cap and bowed to the stairway—to Nelson, Togo and Yamamoto. As we left he bowed again. And as we toured the kamikaze room he was very solemn. Finally we came to the display of the *Yamato*, the great battleship and flagship of the Combined Fleet, which was sent out to its death at the end of the Okinawa campaign in a "kamikaze" effort. Commander Hayashi looked long at the portrait of Admiral Seichi Ito, who accompanied the *Yamato* to her watery grave that summer day of 1945. He related how the admiral had died, although some others were saved. "You know," said Commander Hayashi with pride, "it is the Japanese tradition that a captain always goes down with his ship."

A good deal of pride was evident in the SDF in 1984, and indeed, in all Japan. My interview with the SDF official spokesman, Masuo Morodomi, was conducted, as are all significant exchanges with foreigners, through an interpreter. I noted that Mr. Moridomo several times used the phrase *ware-ware*, which means "we Japanese." So did Kiyohiko Koike, chief administrator of the National Defense Academy. So did Komeito's secretary-general in his address to the party's 1984 convention in Tokyo, which I attended.

Ware-ware has a special meaning far beyond "we Japanese." What it really says is: "We Japanese, the most favored and superior people of the world." Translators do not translate that concept. In the dark days after the surrender *ware-ware* was seldom heard from the military. Its return now to the media and public discussion, along with "Nippon" for Japan, rather than the softer "Nihon"— and "Yamato," an ancient name for Japan—is an indication of a growing national pride. The pride and the movement of Japan toward international power are coming faster now.

In 1984 Japan moved swiftly on the road to rearmament. In the fall, Prime Minister Nakasone promised "to try to keep military spending down to one percent of the gross national product." But by December he was backtracking and his brain-trusters were already indicating that the 1 percent limit should be scrapped in 1985. In December the SDF director appeared on television to tell the nation that Japan's military needs were growing so fast that the limit had become a painful collar.

The argument was that the GNP had become variable—it was down to a 3 percent growth rate in the fall of 1984—and the needs of the military were constant, so the old rules had to be scrapped. That argument was a part of Nakasone's search for consensus. There were still some loose ends to be wrapped up, still some convincing to be done. *Asahi Shimbun*, for example, warned Nakasone to keep defense spending within the 1 percent limitation:

"It is the duty of his cabinet to pursue a policy of peace and international cooperation without blindly following Washington."

Another indication of the speed of movement in the search for consensus is found in a book that was just hitting the Tokyo bookstores in December of 1984: *Beyond War, Japan's Concept of Comprehensive National Security*, by Robert W. Barnett. The book was based partly on a 1980 report to the Japanese cabinet by the former head of the SDF academy, Masamichi Inoki, and partly on one hundred fifty subsequent interviews with prominent people conducted by Mr. Barnett. The book asserted that Japan's proper role in the joint defense effort in the Pacific was to improve its intelligence gathering, and that almost alone. There was something dated about the whole concept by the time the book was published, and about Mr. Inoki's report, which assumed a "demise" of American military and economic superiority, just as the Reagan administration was reasserting both. The interviews ranged from outright pacifism as expressed by the editors of *Nihon Zeizai* (Japan's defense organization should be administered by the United Nations) to outright militarism (Japan should rearm completely without regard to any other nation).

But the government was following its own course, in close cooperation with the United States military. When the city of Fushi ousted its mayor in November of 1984, elections that were construed by many to be a slap against the new military posture (the issue was the building of housing for American troops), the Nakasone government benignly ignored the matter and went on pursuing its consensus.

When a group of Japanese businessmen visited Hawaii that same November they were given a special "strategic briefing" by U.S. Admiral William Crowe, commander-in-chief of the U.S. Pacific forces, with heavy emphasis on the enormous geographic area the Americans had to guard and the difficulties of this policing. The business group was impressed. Admiral Crowe had allies among them: Noboru Goto, president of the Japan Chamber of Commerce and Industry and once a captain in the Imperial Japanese Army, and Rejuzo Sejima, a senior official of C. Itoh and Company and one of Nakasone's main advisors on military matters. During the 1940s Sejima had been Captain Sejima, a career officer at Imperial Headquarters and one of the planners of the war against the United States. He was known to still brood on the Japanese defeat, blaming it on bad strategy in China for the most part. He and Goto agreed that the Japanese were far too complacent about matters of defense. "It would take an actual communist presence in Pusan to awaken the need for defense among our people," Goto said.

That argument was given a new cogency in late November when a "shootout" occurred along the Korean demilitarized zone after North Korean troops moved to chase a Soviet defector who had escaped into South Korea. There were several casualties, and for a time it appeared that the incident might spread into something more serious. Only hours after the affair President Kim Il Sung of the North Korean People's Republic flew to Beijing to confer with the Chinese leaders there. Apparently they were not very comforting, for the incident simmered down.

Nonetheless, the incident and the North Korean state of mind had to be worrisome to the Japanese, particularly in view of the statement made in 1977 by President Jimmy Carter when he indicated almost offhandedly that he might withdraw American troops from Korea—and this apparently without so much as a whisper to Tokyo. That "Korea shock" has not been forgotten. It is reasonable to assume it started Kim Il Sung's acquisitive juices flowing again, as they had flowed in 1950 after Secretary of State Dean Acheson declared that the American defense perimeter did not include South Korea.

Korea continues as the Asian tinderbox. To the Japanese the North Korean ambitions present a dangerous possibility. If the scenario outlined at the opening of this book seems farfetched, let the reader contemplate another:

An incident on the Korean DMZ (demilitarized zone) triggers an invasion by the North Koreans once again, and Kim's troops march south to unify Korea under the communist government. Who is to stop this? The American force in Korea is some forty-one thousand men, as opposed to seven hundred thousand North Korean troops.

Could the Republic of Korea's army of five hundred forty thousand stop the North Koreans? It seems rather doubtful, given the ROK army's history. The world faces another potential Korean crisis, with the basic American help consisting of the third Marine Division in Japanese territory and effective assistance still in the U.S. zone of the interior.

There *is* one strong military force in Asia that is capable of stopping such aggression. It is the Japanese Self-Defense Forces, one hundred fifty-five thousand well-trained ground troops with a high degree of readiness and perhaps the best morale in the world. Drawing on reserves, that force could be augmented very quickly. The catch, at the moment, is that the SDF is constrained by law to operate only in Japanese territory. They could move only if the constitution were changed. And that is the true meaning of businessman Goto's statement at Pearl Harbor. . . . Japan could not look with equanimity on a Korea dominated by a communist government, particularly a North Korea that is the USSR's slavish client state.

In a conversation that dealt in part with the vagaries of American policy in Asia over the years, a high official of the SDF referred back to the "Acheson shock," which the Japanese have always considered to be the root cause of the Korean War of 1950. They have not forgotten, and they continue to look warily on American political policies that can change from administration to administration.

The American attitude, then, is a strong factor in the growing movement in Japan for an increased defense capability. Komeito's Kuroyanogi put the argument this way: The U.S. defense system against Soviet strategic nuclear weapons has been conceived only to protect the United States and so it remains. Kuroyanogi visited the U.S. not long ago, including the North American Air Defense (NORAD) installations and from Japan's point of view he declared the futility of the system. "If an ICBM were launched toward Tokyo from a Soviet base, the period before impact would be twenty-nine minutes. The NORAD defense system would detect the missile, the word would go to the Pentagon, then to the White House, then to Pearl Harbor, then to U.S. forces in Japan, then to the Japanese Self-Defense Force. By that time perhaps thirty minutes would have passed..."

Kuroyanogi smiled, spread his hands, said no more.

Japan feels it must constantly assess the tenor of American opinion and react to it—a feeling that dates from the 1970s when growing American opposition to the Vietnam War forced the U.S. government for the first time in its history to abandon an ally in a war, thereby assuring that ally's defeat.

In Asia the United States is perceived as a not-quite-trustworthy ally in the best of times. Discussing this problem an SDF official was asked what would happen if the U.S. suddenly lapsed into its old isolationist posture.

"Japan would have to defend herself," he said.

That statement of 1984 dramatically indicates how much Japan has changed since 1946, when the framers of the peace constitution "outlawed war forever" and prohibited Japan from establishing defenses.

In 1985 Japan has an army, a navy and an air force, all constitutionally illegal. In fact, Japan has perhaps the most efficiently integrated military organization in the world. There is unlikely to be serious friction among the services when all the senior officers are classmates from the same institution. This closeness, of course, has some built-in dangers. What road the Japanese will travel in the future no one can say exactly, but it is apparent that they are on the move to world military power to match their economic strength, pushed by events. This movement is led by the politicians, not just the military, as Prime Minister Nakasone's initiatives toward China, South Korea and Southeast Asian nations for a Pacific Basin concept indicate. It is a political movement toward a military buildup. As one Japanese told me, if militarism of the old *gunkokushugi* sort ever returns to Japan, it will be brought by the politicians, for there is none so fierce as he who does not have to fight in battle.

POSTSCRIPT

The Japanese language, *Nihongo*, is untranslatable into literal English, as any Japanese will say. It is so full of nuances expressing shades of emotion that the *Japan Times*, a Japanese-owned English-language daily in Tokyo, publishes a column called Nihongo Notes, which has been running in the paper for several years and is so popular that the editors have collected it into booklets. For example, in spoken Japanese several words and phrases appear constantly. One is *desu nee*, which is spoken with an upswing at the end, and coming at the end of a declarative sentence serves to end on a question. "We are going to the beach, *desu nee*?" Or, "We are going to the beach, aren't we?" The purpose is to give the listener a chance to object if he wishes. The speaker does not wish to appear bullying.

The listener then responds to the speaker, often with the word *hai!* interjected at all pauses. *Hai!* serves to tell the speaker that the listener is listening and paying attention to what is said. On a roll call the answer when one's name is called is *hai!*, which in that sense means present and accounted for. So *hai!* is often taken to mean yes, but that is not quite right. There are two perfectly good words for yes: *Aa* and *ee. Hai!* is not quite that. Conceivably one could respond *hai!* and still disagree. The meaning then is: I understand what you are saying and it is just fine. I may disagree but we can go into that later.

That is the strange little word *hai!*

When I visited the National Defense Academy at Yokosuka I was given a copy of the descriptive bulletin Boei Daigaku. On the inside cover of the Japanese edition is printed the "Boei Daigaku Gaksei Ka," the school anthem. I translated it, and when I had finished I took the first verse with me to a meeting with Takehisa Imaizumi, Deputy Chief of the Defense Agency Public Information Division.

Boei Daigaku Gaksei Ka

Umi aoshi taihei no nada
Midori koshi obara no okabe
Manabiya wa hikari kagayoi
Makoto no michi no furusato
Masurao wa yobikai tsudoi
Ashita ni makoto o chikai
Yube ni sokoku o omou
Ishizue koko ni kizukan
Aratanaru hinomoto no tame.

My translation:

The sea is blue, peaceful open sea.
Deep green is Obara hill
 (The site of the Academy)
Where our school gleams beautifully.
May sincerity and truth be our path
Gentlemen, heroes all, we join together.
Tomorrow our binding oath we take
Tonight our land's forefathers come to mind.
Let us copy their ways.
Let the sun rise once again.

After Imaizumi-san had read my translation he smiled. "Yes, you could translate it that way." He pointed out that I had made an error by speaking of Obara hill as "small field hill," a common error because one can learn Japanese proper names (Obara hill) only through experience. He also pointed out that the translation *masu rao* could be "gentlemen" or "heroes," but in this case meant "stouthearted men."

But Imaizumi-san's real objection to my translation came with the last line, "Let the sun rise once again."

"You could translate it that way," he said. "But that is a militarist translation. What I think the song means is, 'Let us build a new Japan.'"

Later I showed my translation to a Japanese teacher friend, and she agreed that the meaning was subject to interpretation. She also felt that what the students meant was "build a new Japan."

That is one of the problems with Nihongo; the words mean what the speaker wants them to mean and much of language has to be construed in context with the speaker's emotional state.

So, if Prime Minister Tojo were to come to life and sing "Aratanaru hinomoto no tame," one would know that he was singing, "Let the sun rise once again," meaning "Let the rising sun rise once again," or "Let Japan once more come to power."

But when Imaizumi-san would sing the song, one would know that he would be singing, "Let us build a new Japan."

The question is: In the years to come, who will be singing the song, and what will be his emotional state?

Hai! Imaizumi-san, hai!

CHAPTER NOTES

1. The Danger

Chapter 1 is a hypothetical projection based on my observations of the Asian scene over more than forty years.

2. The New Militarists

The account of the early days of the U.S. occupation and the Shidehara government's maneuvering comes from several sources, and from observations by the author during this period when he was a correspondent under the SCAP command. Had General MacArthur acceded to the demand that the emperor be tried as a war criminal, the history of Japan would be very different than it has turned out. Quite probably a Socialist government would now be in power. In any event, the stranglehold of the conservative politicians in Japan would have been broken and probably would never have revived. At the same time, the close Japanese-American relationship would never have developed either. Prime Minister Nakasone's attitude toward the Japanese defeat is a matter of record. The maneuverings of the Japanese and the Americans regarding defense are also matters of record. James Auer reported on some of these. The latest reports came in 1984 revelations from Washington about U.S.

National Security Council meetings during which John Foster Dulles and others proposed in the 1950s the rearmament of Japan.

I spent several years in Hawaii in the 1970s and 1980s and was privileged there to meet with several commanders of the U.S. Pacific forces and many members of the staffs. I was thus aware of the growing pressure of defense geography as the Soviets built their Pacific forces in those years. I also had the opportunity to discuss Japanese-American relations and possibilities a number of times with my friend the late John Allison, former U.S. ambassador to Japan.

The Hu Yao-bang–Nakasone meetings were highly publicized in Japan, where they were quite properly seen as the opening of a new chapter in Sino-Japanese relations.

In the summer of 1984 I made a serious effort to secure information and cooperation from the U.S. Department of State in connection with this book. I approached the public affairs section of the department, was referred to the Japan desk and from there to the intelligence section, where a reasonable gentleman named Randolph told me it was an interesting subject and he would be glad to talk to me except that as an intelligence officer he could not speak to a member of the public without permission of someone much higher up. I went back to public affairs and the runaround. Finally a gentleman in the East Asian section of public affairs agreed to talk to me on the telephone, but only to assure me that my whole thesis was foolish and useless. I was, he indicated, the only fool in the world who was concerning himself with this ridiculous idea. I told him I had been reading the writings of some others at the Library of Congress.

"Who?"

"Well, the Russians, for one..."

"What else would you expect?"

"The Indians, for another... the Chinese, and the Japanese themselves..."

"I don't believe that," said the State Department man.

I suggested that he consult the Library of Congress files. When we concluded our conversation, I did not have the feeling he was likely to do so.

"There could never be a revival of Japanese militarism," said he. "Japan has a thoroughly modern military force." And with *that* non sequitur I had to be content, for no more information was forthcoming from the

State Department except handouts of speeches and position papers, including one by an old friend, Harriet Culley. They were enough to show me how little attention was being paid the matter in Washington, a fact I confirmed at the U.S. embassy in Tokyo later in the year. When a friend who works on Capitol Hill related the gist of my tale at a Washington cocktail party, a State Department officer explained that I had been exposed to the big State Department problem. Anyone in the department who spoke to the media, and apparently that included anyone who wrote anything for any sort of publication, was likely to get in trouble with the White House. "Heads roll for things like that," the State Department person said.

3. The Disarmament That Didn't

As the Pacific War ended the United States was really unprepared for peace. Little thought was given to the concept of the postwar world further than the hope that a "United Nations" would somehow control, even help eliminate the basic disagreement that remained in the world after the defeat of the German and Italian dictatorships, the isolation of Franco Spain and the defeat of Japanese militarism. Why anyone would believe that the Soviet Union's leaders had given up their drive for preannounced ambitions seems difficult to understand—but this is with forty years' hindsight. At the time the United Nations concept seemed not only most promising but far more realistic than the old League of Nations, life and expectations reinforced so by the weariness of the Western world after a war that had lasted three and a half years for the United States, six years for Britain, fourteen for China.

Still, the Americans did move swiftly in Japan to prevent what would have been a disaster: USSR occupation of the island of Hokkaido. Almost as soon as the joint occupation of Korea began, MacArthur foresaw that it was going to fail. And the USSR was at least effectively prevented from taking a role in the occupation of Japan.

Also, it did not take America long to learn that the total disarmament of a nation was possible only if the victors were prepared to carry out police functions, including the guarding of the coasts. The Americans were not so prepared in Japan. In the beginning the First Demobilization Ministry (Imperial Army) and the Second Demobilization Ministry (Imperial Navy) were conceived to demobilize Japan. The Japanese professionals resisted, albeit quietly, and in a matter of months the direction changed as the Americans realized that a new threat—seen then as a Soviet-Communist Chinese combine—faced Americans in the Pacific. There was a purge, a handful of Japanese leaders were tried by an international court, using in effect ex-post facto rules, and were convicted of total responsibility for what the Allies termed the Pacific War. As the small marker on their combined memorial in Higashi-Ikebukuro Park in Tokyo says, "To no one's surprise they were executed."

But once that was done, official America's desire for vengeance was satisfied, and the U.S. learned that it had so many new problems in the world that there was little or no time to worry about the old. Japan had to be converted into a Western asset.

Throughout this initial period, which lasted about three years, the Japanese military planners were quiescent, though working to their own ends. Fortunately, from their point of view, although the American occupation brought some unpleasant changes, particularly constitutional, nothing basic was touched; the conservative political alliances remained. As noted in this chapter, a socialist government that managed to secure preliminary support soon lost it, and the conservatives returned to power and *with* the blessing of the American military, which was running the show in Japan. The full story of this revival of conservative power is to be found in the history and reports of SCAP, and in such other works as those of James Auer.

4. A Fertile Field for Militarism

The history of postwar Japan is the story of a nation on a twin-track. The mainstream of Japan flowed in the lanes of commerce. Most Japanese really believed they had eschewed war and military power forever. But all that depended on either living in a peaceful world or having a guardian angel. Japan's guardian angel was the United States, and by the middle 1970s, American ability to shoulder the burdens of the world was slipping, and the American willingness to shoulder them was wearing out. The Americans were moving to the point of insistence that their allies bear a large share of the mutual-defense burdens. As the U.S. saw in Europe, the danger of this tack was that others might not accept the concept of mutuality in the American mold. This was not, however, a problem of the U.S. and Japan in the 1970s nor had it become so by 1985. The U.S. still commanded enormous respect in Japan despite several slips in diplomatic and military acumen. Even so, the handwriting on the wall seemed clear: As Japan took more responsibility for defense, her leaders would demand more authority in making the policies that went with that defense.

Generally speaking, the source material for this chapter is the daily Japanese press, and Hawaii *Hochi*, which monitors the Japanese daily newspapers faithfully and shows in condensed form the complicated life of Japan.

5. The Old Militarists

There are many good histories of the modern Japan that begin with the Meiji restoration. I have used a few of them; see Bibliography. Generally they agree on major trends. Wray and Conroy's *Perspectives on Modern Japanese History* indicates the rethinking by historians of Japan's responsibilities and even of its courses of action in the 1930s and 1940s. Revisionism is the word. And some of the forty-six essays on Japanese history read very much like the statements of the Japanese leaders of the time. Nearly half a century after the events, when the blood has dried, this becomes easier to do.

The Japanese were, are and will be a people with a powerful feeling for the glories of war. But as with so much else, their attitude is peculiar to themselves. The U.S. has its Smithsonian Institution and various military museums. Britain has her Imperial War Museum, where the history of the British Empire is laid out in the exhibition halls. Japan has her Yasukuni Shrine, where it is believed the souls of the 2.5 million "heroic dead" look down upon *kaiten* suicide submarines, *ohka* suicide bombs, guns, and swords and all the implements of war, so placed, say the monks, to remind all visitors of peace.

6. The Rise of the Militarists

Many historians have attempted to explain how Japan got onto the track of militarism in the 1930s, and some of the explanations, though ingenious, are overdone. In 1858 when the Americans stood at the door of Japan, Lord Hatta submitted a memorial to the throne that laid it all out: learn from the foreigners, wait, and when their attention is elsewhere, strike and become the ruler of Asia (see page 000). Viscount Tani virtually repeated the advice in 1887. What that indicates is the constant presence in Japan of an ambitious group of men who sought world leadership. Such a group still exists, and most evident among them is Prime Minister Nakasone. He would never consider himself a militarist in the usual pejorative sense, but that is what the Soviets call him. When considering the future it is best not to rely on the old catchwords but to examine actions and policies and see where they are leading. Prime Minister Nakasone's actions and policies are leading Japan to the position of military power and world influence. Where she will move from there no one can say, but from that point she *might* move to a new imperialism, given the proper conditions.

Niju seifu, the system of double imperial authority that eased the way of the 1930s military clique, does not exist in the 1980s. Neither does the Western feeling of racial superiority over Orientals. The Japanese are largely responsible for this change, in their impressive war effort of the 1940s, their acceptance of defeat and occupation, and their industrial regeneration of the 1960s and 1970s. But what does exist that did not exist in the 1930s is a much more powerful *zaikai*, or system of industrial trusts. Their main interest is in ever expanding the marketplace. In that sense the Japan of the 1980s is much like the Japan of the 1920s. In 1984 the *zaikai*, and the government, began making moves toward China and North Korea to expand the marketplace. Many Japanese businessmen continue to look toward China, as did their fathers, as the ideal marketplace for Japan.

7. The First Conspiracy

The Chinese-Japanese characters at the opening of this chapter mean Sho Wa, Enlightenment and Peace, chosen at the beginning of Emperor Hirohito's reign in 1926 to describe it. General Tanaka, the prime minister in the late 1920s, very nearly carried off the occupation of Manchuria in 1928, but was restrained when the U.S. government warned Japan after the assassination of Manchurian Warlord Chang Tso-lin by the Kwantung Army. The period 1927–1931 saw constant activity by the Young Officers cliques, who were determined that the army would come to power and Manchuria would be Japanese. Ironically, when the Manchurian Incident occurred in 1931, the man the Japanese government sent to stop it was General Tatekawa, the organizer of the Cherry Blossom Society and one of the foremost advocates of Japanese militarism. The failure of the London Naval Conference of 1930 to appease the "fleet faction" of the Japanese navy made it inevitable that they would join the young army officers in seeking the overthrow of civil government. Ironically the Hamaguchi government forced the treaty through, but at the expense of national unity and in so doing set up the almost inevitable bid of the militarists for power.

The events of 1931 go a long way toward explaining what happened in Japan during the next fourteen years, and why. One thing not generally explained in historical accounts of the 1920s was that the "civilian" cabinet officials and other leaders were not ordinary citizens in the American sense. Most of the prime ministers were members of the Japanese nobility. Premier Wakatsuki, for example, was Baron Wakatsuki. Few "ordinary citizens" rose high in the political structure in those years; the "democracy" of Japan was largely illusory even though after 1924 Japan did have universal male suffrage. But the habit of emperor worship and obedience to a master was a definite part of Japanese society and persisted through 1945. When one speaks of civil and military government in Japan in the 1920s and 1930s one is really talking about two groups of the elite; again ironically, the army in that sense was more democratic than the civilian political parties, for through the army a rough-handed peasant boy could rise to even cabinet rank.

In the modern sense, General Sadao Araki was the father of Japanese *bushido*. The concept was purely Japanese and drew upon the way of the samurai in the feudal period. But General Araki led the army in bringing *bushido* and emperor worship to a fever pitch in Japan in the mid-1930s as a part of the militarists' drive for complete power.

Emperor Hirohito has been much maligned. Certainly he made errors, perhaps his worst was in not forcing the prosecution of the Kwantung Army plotters in September, 1931. After that, time ran out swiftly until he became the captive of the militarists. I know that David Bergamini, in his monumental *Imperial Conspiracy*, holds that Hirohito was the real culprit in moving Japan into the hands of the militarists, but more recent scholarship has tended to disprove his conspiracy theory. Hirohito's greatest problem was that he was surrounded by weak advisors who did not come to his aid when he needed them. By the time the Imperial General Headquarters was established in 1937 the militarists had taken total control of Japan, and the forces of moderation were totally submerged. No one really had the courage to stand up and tell the militarists that their course was insane and suicidal, that there was no way Japan could defeat the industrial might of the United States in the long run.

In 1936 Admiral Isoroku Yamamoto was vice-minister of the navy in the Japanese cabinet. He was so outspoken against war with the United States, a course on which the militarists had already embarked, that his friends secured his appointment as Commander of the Combined Fleet because it put him at sea in a battleship, and thus out of the way of the murderous plotters who were ready to assassinate him. Hence Yamamoto, the foremost military opponent of the war, was put in the position of having to prosecute it against the enemy he knew he could never defeat.

8. The New Militarism: The Self-Defense Forces

Most of this chapter derives from my study of the Japanese media during the summer and autumn of 1984, after Prime Minister Nakasone announced that he would seek to secure a consensus favoring Japanese rearmament on a larger and swifter basis than the past. The American embassy in Tokyo was certainly aware of the Japanese government's activities, the problems and the long-range dangers of Japanese rearmament. But that awareness, it would seem, had not trickled down to the State Department.

The answer, then, has to be that while one can believe anything one learns at the U.S. embassy in Tokyo, what comes out of the State Department in Washington is self-serving to the administration and often incredible.

9. The Spirit of Japan: Military

Like the Americans, the Japanese love public opinion polls, and scarcely a week goes by in Tokyo that one is not published. The government watches them closely. In 1985 public opinion polls were a key to the rate of success of the Nakasone government's search for national support of greater rearmament. Yukio Mishima will soon be lionized once again in Japan. A French filmmaker in 1984 was recreating Mishima. Of course the filmmaker spoke no Japanese, so what comes out will be his own version, as affected by the Japanese who influenced him, not likely to have much relationship to the real Mishima but very likely to further the ultranationalist image. One of the phenomena of the 1980s is the breakdown of the pacifist phalange, as exemplified by the turnabout of Professor Ikutaro Shimizu. For all practical purposes in 1984 the pacifist movement was dead; even the Socialists had accepted the need for the defense force. And as for the men who serve, they could very easily meet the standards of the old Meiji Soldiers and Sailors Creed; their own standards are derived from it and remain the same in essence (see Appendixes).

10. The Spirit of Japan: Political

By the end of 1985 the question of the three nuclear no's for Japan was moot. The pacifists would continue to discuss them, but all political parties had in some way accommodated themselves to the fact that the American nuclear umbrella over Japan rested on nuclear missiles aboard American ships. As one Komeito politician put it, "We say certain things for public consumption, just as do George Schultz and President Reagan. We know the facts, and so do they."

The situation of the Yasukuni Shrine is unique in Japan. It is a national shrine dedicated to peace, and it is still operated as if Shintoism were the official Japanese religion. The grounds are studied with implements of war as is its museum—a nice example of the complex duality of the Japanese toward war and peace.

11. Articles of Faith

The question of religion is never far below the surface in Japan, as anyone who visits a Shinto shrine or a Buddhist temple will note. The Japanese are inveterate tourists, their own country is their favorite touring ground and their lack of self-consciousness as they approach the altar, make a prayer, drop a contribution and clap their hands is remarkable to witness. Religion is not a compartment in Japanese lives as it is with Westerners who set certain days and certain hours for consideration of the faith. This chapter speaks largely of the religion and attitudes of the past, but I hope it also shows how easy it would be for the past to repeat itself in a society which in its religious aspects is so little changed in half a century.

12. Japan in Search of Itself

In his death throes Admiral Takejiro Ohnishi, the father of the kamikazes, did not believe he would be forgotten in Japan. And he has not been. The suicide divers of World War II are the most highly honored of all Japanese heroes, the level of adulation is that bestowed on the most famous of the admirals and generals. There is no sense of apology in the exhibits at the service academy museums and at the great Yasukuni Shrine.

At the service academies the students are taught that it is their mission to help create a "new Japan" and they are doing so, as the Defense Academy song says, "while honoring our forefathers."

13. The New Industrial Power

The *zaikai*, or modern industrial cartels, are very much the children of the *zaibatsu*, only bigger and stronger, more numerous and more versatile. They are the secret of Japan's success, but they could not possibly be transferred to any other social structure.

There is one major difference between the *zaikai* of the 1980s and the *zaibatsu* of the 1930s: The modern *zaikai* have made of Japan a great economic power without military assistance. The *zaibatsu* were dragged along by the military and dominated by them. That is why if militarism takes over Japan it will have to come through the politicians.

14. Through the Looking Glass: The U.S., Japan and the Pacific

I grew up in Portland, Oregon, learning in the public schools that the United States was not and had never been an imperialist power. Indeed I was taught that America had always opposed imperialism, and the great example was the Open Door in China and our refusal to accept compensation after the Boxer Rebellion. I did not study Far Eastern affairs in the university so it was only after I got out into the world that I learned that my historical education had been in large degree eyewash.

The point is, of course, that all peoples are exposed to the sort of education their government, their tradition, want them to have. One nation's history is another nation's fairy tale. What American officialdom too often fails to understand is that the Japanese and American views are destined to be different; the American responsibility is to ascertain the real Japanese views (as opposed to politesse) and to be guided by them in formulating our policy. Fortunately, in 1985 the U.S. is blessed with an almost uniquely prescient ambassador to Japan, Mike Mansfield. So if Washington is going astray, it will not be for lack of information and guidance from the man in the field.

15. Are the Words of the Past the Words of the Future?

I have included these many quotations from the Japanese past and present to show the reader how words change and yet remain the same. To me, two of the quotations stand out as prophetic and up-to-date even now—those of Lord Hatta in 1858 and Viscount Tani twenty years later. They represent the national feeling of a powerful and ambitious people. The Japanese did not change, and in the twentieth century they took advantage of their "opportunities" but overplayed their hand. That is not likely to happen to them again; one of the reasons for Japan's behavior in the 1940s was the enormous ignorance of the Japanese army generals of the real sources of world power and the potential strength of the United States. The Japanese military of the 1980s is far better educated in weltpolitik. But the Japanese beliefs in Japan and her place in the world have not changed nearly as much as many seem to believe.

16. Japan Rearms

The Japan of the 1980s is very much like the Japan of the 1920s, a newly emerged world power not quite certain of its proper course. Within Japan are elements moving to defuse the military by economic expansion. Japan in 1985 has one of the most far-reaching foreign aid programs of any nation in the world. The attempt, quite conscious in Tokyo, was to prove international goodwill and strengthen Japan's moral position as she moved out in search of more markets. Those who complain about that aggressiveness are, one suspects, shortsighted, because Japan, by and large, has only one national asset, and that is the enormous vigor of her people. If this cannot be turned profitably to trade, it will be turned in other directions, as it was in the 1930s.

APPENDIX A

Imperial Rescript to Soldiers and Sailors

From the Meiji restoration until the Japanese surrender in 1945 all Japanese soldier and sailor recruits (and later many students) were ordered to memorize this entire rescript. Several times a year and on all formal occasions the rescript was read to the troops in official ceremony, lest in any way it become less than gospel to them. It should be studied by Westerners with care:

The forces of Our Empire are in all ages under the command of the Emperor. It is more than twenty-five centuries since the Emperor Jimmu, leading in person the soldiers of the Otomo and Mononobe clans, subjugated the unruly tribes of the land and ascended the Imperial throne to rule over the whole country. During this period the military system has undergone frequent changes in accordance with those of the state of society. In ancient times the rule was that the Emperor should take personal command of the forces; and although the military authority was sometimes delegated to the Empress or the Prince Imperial, it was scarcely ever entrusted to a subject. In the Middle Ages, when the civil and military institutions were framed after the Chinese model, the Six Guards were founded, the Right and Left Horse Bureaus established, and other organizations such as that of the Coast Guards, created. The military system was thus created, but habituated to a prolonged state of peace,

231

the Imperial Court gradually lost its administrative vigor; in course of time soldiers and farmers became distinct classes, and the early conscription system was replaced by an organization of volunteers, which finally produced the military class. The military power passed over entirely to the leaders of this class; through disturbances in the Empire the political power also fell into their hands; and for about seven centuries the military families held sway. Although these results followed from changes in the state of society and were deeply to be deplored, since they were contrary to the fundamental character of Our Empire and to the law of Our Imperial Ancestors. Later on, in the eras of Kokwa and Kaei, the decline of the Tokugawa Shogunate and the new aspect of foreign relations even threatened to impair our national dignity, causing no small anxiety to Our August Grandfather, the Emperor Ninko, and Our August Father, the Emperor Komei, a fact which We recall with awe and gratitude. When in youth we succeeded to the Imperial Throne, the Shogun returned into Our hands the administrative power, and all the feudal lords and their fiefs; thus in a few years, Our entire realm was unified and the ancient regime restored. Due as this was to the meritorious service of Our loyal officers and wise councillors, civil and military, and to the abiding influence of Our Ancestors' benevolence toward the people, yet it must also be attributed to Our subjects' true sense of loyalty and their conviction of the importance of "Great Righteousness." In consideration of these things, being desirous of reconstructing Our military system and enhancing the glory of Our Empire, We have, in the course of the last fifteen years, established the present system of the Army and Navy. The supreme command of Our force is in Our hands, and although We may entrust subordinate commands to Our subjects, yet the ultimate authority We Ourself shall hold and never delegate to any subject. It is Our will that this principle be carefully handed down to posterity and that the Emperor always remain the supreme civil and military power, so that the disgrace of the middle and succeeding ages may never be repeated. Soldiers and Sailors, We are your supreme Commander in Chief. Our relations with you will be most intimate when We rely on you as Our limbs and you look up to Us as your head. Whether We are capable to guard the Empire and so prove Ourself worthy of Heaven's blessing and repay the benevolence of Our Ancestors depends on the faithful discharge of your duties as soldiers and sailors. If the majesty and power of Our Empire be impaired, do you share with Us the sorrow;

if the glory of Our arms shine resplendent, We will share with you the honor. If you all do your duty, and being one with Us in spirit do your utmost for the protection of the State, Our people will long enjoy the blessings of peace, and the might and dignity of Our Empire will shine in the world. As We expect much of you, Soldiers and Sailors, We give you the following precepts:

1. The soldier and sailor should consider loyalty their essential duty. Who that is born in this land can be wanting in the spirit of grateful service to it? No soldier or sailor, especially, can be considered efficient unless this spirit is strong within him. A soldier or sailor in whom this spirit is not strong, however skilled in art or proficient in science, is a mere puppet; and a body of soldiers or sailors wanting in loyalty, however well ordered and disciplined it may be is in an emergency no better than a rabble. Remember that as the protection of the State and the maintenance of its power depend upon the strength of its arms, the growth or decline of this strength must affect the nation's destiny for good or for evil; therefore neither be led astray by current opinions nor meddle in politics, but with single heart fulfill your essential duty of loyalty, and bear in mind that duty is weightier than a mountain, while death is lighter than a feather. Never by failing in moral principles fall into disgrace and bring dishonor upon your name.

2. The soldier and the sailor should be strict in observing propriety. Soldiers and sailors are organized in grades, from the Marshal and the Admiral of the Fleet down to the private soldier or ordinary seaman; and even within the same rank and grade there are differences in seniority of service according to which juniors should submit to their seniors. Inferiors should regard the orders of their superiors as issuing directly from Us. Always pay due respect not only to your superiors but also to your seniors, even though not serving under them. On the other hand, seniors should not treat their juniors with contempt or arrogance. Except when official duty requires them to be strict, and severe, superiors should treat their inferiors with consideration, making kindness their chief aim, so that all grades may unite in their service to the Emperor. If you, Soldiers and Sailors, neglect to observe propriety, treating your superiors with disrespect and your inferiors with harshness, and thus cause harmonious cooperation to be lost, you will not only be a blight upon the forces but also be unpardonable offenders against the State.

3. The soldier and the sailor should esteem valor. Ever since the ancient

times valor has in our country been held in high esteem, and without it Our subjects would be unworthy of their name. How, then, may the soldier and the sailor, whose profession it is to confront the enemy in battle, forget for even one instant to be valiant? But there is true valor and false. To be incited by mere impetuosity to violent action cannot be called true valor. The soldier and the sailor should have sound discrimination of right and wrong, cultivate self-possession, and form their plans with deliberation. Never to despise an inferior enemy or fear a superior, but to do one's duty as soldier or sailor—this is true valor. Those who thus appreciate true valor should in their daily intercourse set gentleness first and aim to win the love and esteem of others. If you affect valor and act with violence, the world will in the end detest you and look upon you as wild beasts. Of this you should take heed.

4. The soldier and the sailor should highly value faithfulness and righteousness. Faithfulness and righteousness are the ordinary duties of man, but the soldier and the sailor, in particular, cannot be without them and remain in the ranks even for a day. Faithfulness implies the keeping of one's word and righteousness the fulfillment of one's duty. If then you wish to be faithful and righteous in anything, you must carefully consider at the outset whether you can accomplish it or not. If you thoughtlessly agree to do something that is vague in its nature and bind yourself to unwise obligations, and then try to prove yourself faithful and righteous, you may find yourself in great straits from which there is no escape. In such cases your regret will be of no avail. Hence you must first make sure whether the thing is righteous and reasonable or not. If you are convinced that you cannot possibly keep your word and maintain righteousness, you had better abandon your engagement at once. Ever since the ancient times there have been repeated instances of great men and heroes who, overwhelmed by misfortune, have perished and left a tarnished name to posterity, simply because in their effort to be faithful in small matters, they failed to discern right and wrong with reference to fundamental principles, or because, losing sight of the true path of public duty, they kept faith in private relations. You should, then, take serious warning by these samples.

5. The soldier and the sailor should make simplicity their aim. If you do not make simplicity your aim, you will become effeminate and frivolous and acquire fondness for luxurious and extravagant ways; you will finally grow selfish and sordid and sink to the last degrees of baseness,

so that neither loyalty nor valor will avail to save you from the contempt of the world. It is not too much to say that you will thus fall into a lifelong misfortune. If such an evil once makes its appearance among soldiers and sailors, it will certainly spread like an epidemic, and martial spirit and morale will instantly decline. Although being greatly concerned on this point, We lately issued the Disciplinary Regulations and warned you against this evil, nevertheless, being harassed with anxiety lest it should break out, We hereby reiterate Our warning. Never do you, Soldiers and Sailors, make light of this injunction.

These five articles should not be disregarded even for a moment by soldiers and sailors. Now for putting them to practice, the all important is sincerity. These five articles are the soul of Our soldiers and sailors, and sincerity is the soul of these articles. If the heart be not sincere, words and deeds, however good, are all mere outward show and can avail nothing. If only the heart be sincere, anything can be accomplished. Moreover, these articles are The Grand Way of heaven and Earth and the universal law of humanity, easy to observe and to practice. If you, Soldiers and Sailors, in obedience to Our instruction, will observe and practice these principles and fulfil your duty of grateful service to the country, it will be a source of joy, not to Ourself alone, but to the people of Japan.

The 4th day of the last month of the 15th Year of Meiji [January 4, 1880]

Meiji

APPENDIX B

Oath taken upon entering the National Defense Academy:

I do hereby swear that, with a full understanding of the honor and responsibility of the Cadet of the National Defense Academy, I will obey the Constitution of Japan, laws and ordinances, together with the regulations of the Academy, cultivate my character, respect the personality of others, train my body and mind, enrich my knowledge in every field, and concentrate all my energy to the works without any concern for, and participation in, any political activities.

APPENDIX C

Moral Education

The Imperial Naval Academy's Five Reflections
  1. Hast Thou not gone against sincerity?
  2. Hast thou not felt ashamed of thy words and deeds?
  3. Hast thou not lacked vigor?
  4. Hast thou exerted all possible effort?
  5. Hast thou not become slothful?

BIBLIOGRAPHY

Books

Agawa, Hiroyuki. *The Reluctant Admiral*. Tokyo: Kodansha International, 1979.

Auer, James E. *The Postwar Rearmament of Japanese Maritime Forces, 1945–71*. New York: Praeger Publishers, 1973.

Causten, E. E. N. *Militarism and Foreign Policy in Japan*. London: George Allen and Unwin, 1937.

Christopher, Robert C. *The Japanese Mind*. New York: Fawcett Columbine, 1983.

Colegrove, Kenneth W. *Militarism in Japan*. Boston: World Peace Foundation, 1936.

Emmerson, John K. and Leonard A. Humphreys. *Will Japan Rearm*. Washington: American Enterprise Institute for Public Policy Research, 1973.

Fujiwara, Hirotatsu. *I Denounce Soka Gakkai*. Tokyo: Nisshin Hodo Co., 1970.

Fukuchi, Shigetaka. *Gunkoku Nihon no Keisei; Shizoku Ishiki Tenkai to sono Shumatsu*. Tokyo: Haruaki Sha, 1960.

Gomigawa, Jumpei. *Kyokugen Jokyo ni Okeru Ninjin*. Tokyo: Takemura, 1973. Banin

Hoyt, Edwin P. *The Kamikazes*. New York: Arbor House, 1983.

———. *Pacific Destiny*. New York: W. W. Norton Co., 1982.

———. *The Russo-Japanese War*. New York: Abelard Schuman, 1966.

Kataoka, Tetsuya. *Waiting for a Pearl Harbor*. Stanford, Calif.: Hoover Institution Press, 1980.

Krauss, Ellis S., Thomas P. Rohlen, and Patricia G. Steinhoff, eds. *Conflict in Japan*. Honolulu: University of Hawaii Press, 1984.

Latourette, Kenneth Scott. *The Development of Japan*. New York: Macmillan, 1938.

Lory, Hillis. *Japan's Military Masters*. Washington: The Infantry Journal Press, 1943.

Lyons, Graham, ed. *The Russian Version of the Second World War*. New York: Facts on File, 1976.

Minichiello, Sharon. *Retreat from Reform. Patterns of Political Behavior in Interwar Japan*. Honolulu: University of Hawaii Press, 1984.

Norman, E. Herbert. *Soldiers and Peasants in Japan*. New York: Institute of Pacific Relations, 1943.

Quigley, Harold S. *Far Eastern War, 1937–1941*. Boston: World Peace Foundation, 1943.

Reischauer, Edwin O. *Japan: Past and Present*. Boston: Houghton Mifflin, 1947.

Sansom, G. B. *Japan: A Short Cultural History*. New York: Appleton Century, 1943.

Shiratori, Rei., ed. *Japan in the 1980s*. Tokyo: Kodansha International Ltd., 1982.

Shiroyama, Saburo. *War Criminal, the Life and Death of Hirota Koki*. Tokyo: Kodansha International, 1974.

Shokawa, Taro, ed. *Gunkoku Shugi Kyoiku #3, Gunkoku Shugi to Minshuteki Kyoiku*. Tokyo: Fujiowara Seiyu, 1970.

Shuppanbu, Chauo i inkai, Nihon Kyosanto, eds. *Fukkatsu suru nihon Gunkaku shugi*. Tokyo: Nihon Kyosanto Chuo i inkai Shuppanbu, 1966.

Sunoo, Harold Hakwon. *Japanese Militarism, Past and Present*. Chicago: Nelson-Hall, Inc., 1975.

Suzuki, Daisetz T. *Zen and Japanese Culture*. Princeton: Princeton University Press.

Takeyama, Michio. *The Spirit of Our Times*. Trans. by J. A. Harrison. Gainesville, Fla.: University of Florida Department of History, 1958. Published in Japan as *Showa no Seishinshi*, 1950.

Tanin, O. and E. Yohan. *Militarism and Fascism in Japan.* New York: International Publishers, 1934.

Tolischus, Otto D. *Through Japanese Eyes.* New York: Reynal & Hitchcock, 1975.

Turnbull, S. R. *Samurai, A Military History.* New York: Macmillan, 1977.

Wray, Harry and Hilary Conroy. *Japan Examined, Perspectives on Modern Japanese History.* Honolulu: University of Hawaii Press, 1983.

Zhukov, Y. M., ed. *The Rise and Fall of the Gumbatsu.* Moscow: Progress Publishers, 1975.

Newspapers

Asahi Shimbun
Asahi Evening News
Hawaii Hochi
Japan Times
Mainichi Shimbun
Mainichi Daily
Yomiuri Shimbun
Yomiuri Daily

Articles

Auer, Lt. Cdr. J.E. "Japanese Militarism." *United States Naval Institute Proceedings*, September, 1979, pp. 46–55.

Burkman, Thomas. "The Paradox of Pacifism and Powerhood in the Japanese League of Nations Movement." *Peace & Change*, Winter, 1980, pp. 43–48.

De Roy, Swadesh R. "Prospects for Militarism in Japan." *Pacific Community*, January, 1974, pp. 289–302.

Editors, *Japan Quarterly.* "Militarism. No!" *Japan Quarterly*, April–June, 1972, pp. 132–139.

Eikenberry, Karl W. "The Japanese Defense Debate, A Growing Consensus." *Parameters*, June, 1982, pp. 69–78.

Flemington, Peter. "To Remember the Fallen: Conflict in Japan." *Liberty*, July–August, 1980, pp. 2–26.

Fraser, Angus M. "Some Thoughts on the Resurgence of Militarism in

Japan." *Pacific Community*, April, 1973, pp. 437–451.

Gekkan Economisuto. "The Evolution of Japan's Defense Plans." *The Japan Interpreter*, Spring, 1973, pp. 214–218.

Gomikawa, Junpei. "Rethinking Showa's Half Century." *The Japan Interpreter*, Spring, 1973, pp. 352–353.

Kirk, Donald. "The Possible Future Japan Chooses to Ignore." *World View*, August, 1974, pp. 13–16.

Kobayashi, Keiji. "An Asian Image of Japan." *The Japan Interpreter*, Spring, 1972, pp. 129–137.

Kojima, Noburo. "Militarism and the Emperor System." *The Japan Interpreter*, Spring, 1973, pp. 219–227.

Kotani, Hidejiro. "Views on the Resurgence of Militarism." *The Japan Interpreter*, Spring, 1973, pp. 195–204.

Masakuni, Kitazawa. "Militarism Under the Cloak of Management Society." *The Japan Interpreter*, Spring, 1973 pp. 324–328.

Matsuzawa, Tetsunaru. "Ishiwara Kanji to Sekai Saishu Sen, Ron ichi" ("Ishiwara Kanji and the Ultimate War, Argument 1"). *Shokai Kozaku Kenkyu*, Vol. 22, No. 3, 1971, pp. 95–162.

———. "Ron ni," *Shokai Kozaku Kenkyu*, Vol. 22, No. 4, 1971, pp. 45–116.

Matthews, Ron G. "Japanese Militarism, A British Perspective." *Revista Internazionale de Scienze Economiche e Commercialici*, Luglio, 1982, pp. 700–720.

Mazhorov, S. "Japan on the Road to Militarism." (Translation) *Voyenno-Istoricheskiy Zhurnal*, No. 2, February, 1971, pp. 39–46.

McNelly, Theodore. "Disarmament and Civilian Control in Japan, A Constitutional Dilemma." *Bulletins of Peace Proposals*, Vol. 13, No. 4, 1982, pp. 351–364.

Mendl, Wolf. "The Japan Constitution and Japan's Security Policy." *Millenium, Journal of International Studies*, Spring, 1978, pp. 36–51.

Muccia, Lt. Daniel E. "Japanese Militarism." Letter in *U.S. Naval Institute Proceedings*, February, 1974, pp. 90–94.

Osamu, Inagaki. "The Jieitai: Military Values in a Pacifist Society?" *Japan Interpreter*, Summer, 1975, pp. 1–15.

Panda, Rajaram. "Security Concerns and Militarism in Japan." *Asia Pacific Community*, Spring, 1983, pp. 20–34.

Powles, Cyril. "Yasukuni Jinja Hoan: Religion and Politics in Contemporary Japan." *Pacific Affairs*, Fall, 1946, pp. 491–505.

Pronin, V. "The Defeat of Japanese Militarism and Changes in the Far East." *International Affairs*, October, 1975, pp. 33–41.

Savin, A. "The Aggressiveness of the Japanese Militarists." (Translation.) *Voyenno-Istoricheskiy Zhurnal*, No. 8, August, 1980, pp. 68–75.

Sheldon, Charles D. "Japanese Aggression and the Emperor, 1931–1941, from Contemporary Diaries." *Modern Asian Studies*, No. 10, 1976, pp. 1–40.

Shinkichi, Etoo. "Japan and America in Asia During the Seventies." *The Japan Interpreter*, Spring, 1972, pp. 245–254.

Sidorov, A. Col. "The Rout of Japanese Militarism." *Voyenno-Istoricheskiy Zhurnal*. (Translation.) No. 8, August, 1980, pp. 11–16.

Swomley, John M., Jr. "Militarism Returns to Japan." *The Christian Century*, February 12, 1974, pp. 176–178.

Takuji, Shimano. "Economic Growth and the Rise of Militarism." *The Japan Interpreter*, Spring, 1973, pp. 205–213.

Yamamura, Kozo. "Meiji Militarism." *The Journal of Economic History*, March, 1977, pp. 113–138.

Pamphlets, etc.

Kinji Kawamura. *Japan, A Pocket Guide*. Tokyo: Foreign Press Center, 1984.

White paper. *Defense of Japan*. Tokyo: Defense Agency, 1983.

White paper. *Defense of Japan*. Tokyo: Defense Agency, 1984.

Public Information Division Defense Bulletin. Tokyo: Defense Agency, 1982.

Teruhiko Onabe. *An Introduction to Japanese History*. Tokyo: Foreign Press Center, 1983.

Boei Cho. *Boei Daigaku*. Tokyo: Nihon Boei Cho, 1984.

Index

247